ROSARIO'S GETTING OUT

ROSARIO'S GETTING OUT

IT'S PAYBACK TIME

A Novel

STEPHEN SCHNITZER

iUniverse, Inc.
Bloomington

Rosario's Getting Out
It's Payback Time

iUniverse books may be ordered through booksellers or by contacting:

iUniverse
1663 Liberty Drive
Bloomington, IN 47403
www.iuniverse.com
1-800-Authors (1-800-288-4677)

ISBN: 978-1-4697-8290-4 (sc)
ISBN: 978-1-4697-8291-1 (hc)
ISBN: 978-1-4697-8289-8 (e)

Library of Congress Control Number: 2012903384

Printed in the United States of America

iUniverse rev. date: 02/16/2012

Dedication

To all my friends and clients who have done hard time.

    To my beloved wife, Jo-Ann, and my daughter, Jennifer, who can still hear the ringing of the prison doors slamming after five years treating inmates as a doctor of psychology for the US Department of Prisons in Butner, North Carolina.

    Finally to my friend and pal, Bentley, who has been the mainstay of encouragement for this and all prior works. Traditionally, as before, he slept nearby or tried to criminally attack his toy dogs as a constant reminder that crime never sleeps.

Cast of Characters

Honorable R. Homer Barrett Jr – presiding judge, Jackson municipal court

Wilber Armstrong, Esq. – public defender, Jackson, Mississippi

Ruben L. Staggers, Esq. – state's attorney

Honorable Reginald Stittin – chief criminal judge, Jackson, Mississippi

Taylor Hawkins, Esq. – public defender, trial section, Jackson, Mississippi

Vickie Trucker – former go-go bar dancer and surprise witness

Warden Cain Kikes – warden, Mississippi State Prison, Biloxi, Mississippi

Assistant Warden Taylor – assistant warden, Mississippi State Prison, Biloxi, Mississippi

Joshua– the warden's fourteen-year-old son

Sara – the warden's twelve-year-old daughter

Julie – Holiday Inn concierge and later a friend to Rosario

Mr. Goldstien – tailor and later a friend to Rosario

Hans Gruber – private banker to Rosario, Zurich, Switzerland

Arnot Sinclair – banker, First National Bank of Mississippi

Louis, Kroper, Frenchy – legionnaire friends of Rosario

Grace Trouller – real estate broker, Jackson, Mississippi

Stephanie – second-in-command to Julie at the Mansion.

Ross Gillmore II – the former governor's son and the lawyer to the mysterious purchaser for the Mansion

Mr. Luther Helms III – Ku Klux Klan wizard and formal director

Mrs. Luther Helms III— Mansion regular and the prosperous wife of Luther Helms III

Prologue

He was not short or tall, yet he did not look like an average person. He was wiry, very wiry, and it made him look thin and perhaps weak to the untrained eye. Instead, he was anything but average or passively mild. His appearance was part of his deception; it was his practiced presentation.

He had flown into Jackson, Mississippi's airport nearly eight hours before, deplaned, and started his walk, backpack in hand. He wore khaki pants, hiking boots, a plaid red flannel shirt, and a small peaked cap with a large front bill to keep the sun off his face. All of his clothes were well worn and showed no signs of affluence.

He moved along at a quick but easy pace, almost as though he was marching in a military parade. His blue eyes and blond hair, lightened by long hours in a climate with a hot sun, complemented his deeply tanned complexion. Together, they enhanced his appearance. He was clearly a man women would agree was virile and attractive. "Manly" would be the best description.

Actually, he had come for the women. He intended to hike the Natchez Trace into the Creole bayous of Mississippi and Louisiana, searching for a good-hearted woman to marry and start a family with. She would speak French, even if in the Creole dialect. He felt that he could even linger for several months if he believed he had found the right one, spending time to be certain. It could not be a quick, overnight process. A marriage was meant to last. He wanted his best opportunity at it. A few weeks would not do, and even months later, the best proposal might be marginal: live together for a while and see how it worked. That was nothing unusual in these times, although he knew the girl's family (if she had one) might oppose it. Creoles were old school. It was not a test. If he knew it was right, he would take the step of marriage, but if he was not sure, he would try to see if the relationship worked. He could afford to do so, because money was not a factor, but he did not want to show his financial strength, so it would not be of influence. Such were the thoughts that busied his mind as he hiked forward.

He began to look for a roadside place to eat near woods where he could camp for the night. Time passed, and he marched on, passing a small gas station, the occasional roadside home, and a hilltop with a small, stark white church that struck him as particularly spectacular with the cross on its small steeple blaring like an emblem sewn onto the apron of the descending, late–September afternoon sun. Nothing was moving about it on this Saturday evening. There were no worshipers seeking to avoid Sunday morning prayers by getting it all over with the night before to stay in grace. That image would repeat itself time and time again in the future months, but he was not foreseeing enough to know it. The worst was yet to come.

He found a diner four miles south and more than an hour later and stopped to feed himself. He was in no hurry, so he ate at the diner slowly. Then he took coffee in a cup for the morning and cornbread to eat. He bought a quart of water to see him through the night if he found no stream and tipped the waitress well. She chatted with him about where he was going and how to make his way farther south to join the trace itself. Everyone was happy. Rosario was at peace.

He entered a wood locked roadside opening and made a quick bed of leaves, covering it with a light knapsack blanket. He drifted off until sunlight would wake him. He had no suspicion of pending doom.

CHAPTER ONE

Le Petite Monsieur

The little man was just that: little. But he was manlike even as a child. He spent most of his social time in the company of adults, speaking freely with them as they replied to him. Age was not a factor—thought and intelligence were the medium of exchange. By eight, Rosario could hold his own, giving his opinions freely and replying to those of his elders, whether they were relatives or not.

His father and mother married late. His father was forty and his mother thirty-five. His parents were of mixed nationality, but both were ethnic Jews. His mother was American born, and she grew up on Long Island in the elegant section of Kings Point on the water, scant blocks from the Coast Guard Academy. Her father had been a prosperous developer who built custom-made villas for successful New York businessmen and professionals who flocked yearlong from the city for extended weekends of relative peace.

His father's family was expatriated German and Jewish. The family left the comfort of Berlin after Kristallnacht and Hitler's then recent ascent to chancellor. They had thought that France was far enough away, and their son, Rosario's father, was born in early 1943 at the height of the war. Almost immediately thereafter, the French Jews were rounded up en masse, and Rosario's father was placed to be raised as the putative child of

Catholic antique dealers. His parents were denounced and carted off. Both died en route, robbing the gas chamber of its claims on them. The young Rosario heard the story only once from his father. It did not come up again. It was not a topic of discussion within the small family of three.

After the war years, the French had a change of heart regarding Jews and inspired them to join government service, preferring to trust them over more native Frenchmen who had earlier dallied with the Nazi's, becoming their partisans. They also accepted that Jews were somehow inherently smarter and more suited to matters of discipline and intelligence services.

After completing his schooling, Rosario's father was sought out by the Suretee. He enlisted and trained in general police matters. When he obviously excelled in his studies and became noted for being just plain smart, he was routed into the intelligence division and designated for foreign service. In this manner, he developed his career and was assigned to embassies and delegations in Europe and finally in the United States to the French delegation to the United Nations. It was on this assignment in New York City that he met and later married Rosario's mother with whom he returned to France, having been promoted both in rank and in a management position within the secret service of France.

The only condition his mother had placed on their marriage was that, from the age of three on, their young boy would spend summers stateside with her parents, who doted on him as their only grandchild. The boy came along a few years later. The French school recess was shorter than that in the United States, which allowed the boy almost three months of vacation annually. During these trips, he perfected his English, learning to think in the language and speak it like a native without an accent as he spoke French when at home. His maternal grandfather was an avid outdoorsman who took the boy to hunt and fish for weeks at a time, camping out in Maine and western Massachusetts. They hiked the summer woods and climbed the taller mountains, like Greylock. When the boy got older, they climbed in the Rockies and the Grand Canyon. Rosario learned to love the outdoors and enjoy the confidence of a woodsman, moving freely in the outdoors, understanding the nature of plants and animals. Early on, he learned the woodsman's tricks and the rules of wilderness survival. These lessons never left him.

By the age of ten, the boy was becoming the French equivalent of an army brat, moving time and time again with his parents to yet another foreign posting. His father spent long hours at work with executive duties, and his mother had little to do with a lot of help. Her burdens became charity work and the entertaining of other French families that were similarly posted. To avoid more upheaval, Rosario's parents agreed that he should have stability with a regular school environment without constant schooling disruptions from the threefold or more yearly relocations. He was placed in a Swiss boarding school within the Zurich Canton. He was educated in French, Swiss, and English and learned to read and study in all three.

Even as a younger man, Rosario perfected the art of reading, in part because there were few family adventures because his parents remained constantly busy with their own affairs, which made him somewhat feral. The boy loved to read, learn, and experience, even if vicariously, the events and places that rose out of the turned page. These lessons in life stretched his insight and exercised his mind.

His European school experiences also stressed travel and physical capacity. The boy learned to climb the Alps, to ski, and to hike and travel in the woods alone as he had in earlier days with his grandfather. He did not compete with others so much as with himself in developing his skills of self-reliance and his physical ability, dovetailing them with his already accomplished mental development. In this manner, he was strengthened to weather tragedy.

When he was fifteen, his parents were reposted by the ministry to Algeria, once a favored son of France. Now it had deteriorated into an unruly child, broken by subversive terrorist activities of rebels, dissidents, and separatists. His father had been so assigned because he was credited with being a minor hero in Algeria, which favored almost no white Frenchmen at the time.

Due to his repeated postings and constant concern for the security of government members developed through his intelligence work, he studied protection needs and defects both obvious and subtle. He reached a simple conclusion. During a terrorist event it was difficult in the heat of the moment to tell a friend from a foe, especially when the enemy was wearing your garb. You ended up disoriented, shooting both friend and foe alike, helping to flame the overall disruption the enemy desired.

The Algerians were an elegant and distinguished people, including visually. Obviously, they spoke the king's French. Many were born soldiers, in great physical shape, and nearly as tall as Maasai warriors. Like Jews, one Algerian knew another across a crowded room. Thus, the solution his father divined was simple and easily adopted throughout France in its government facilities. As early as the 1980s, he installed Gurka-like Algerians who were fully trained in antiterrorism as the official palace guard and in all government buildings. They lived together, ate together, bunked together, and protected together. In the few instances when there was trouble, they did not kill each other but rather operated effectively as a trained military unit. His father's trust of these Algerian soldiers and the ability of well over several thousand native families to prosper and achieve while they were in the military made him popular when he was assigned to North Africa.

It also made him a terrorist target. He and his wife were assassinated in Algiers while returning late at night from a diplomatic consular affair. They were blown apart in their armored vehicle by light rocket fire, just like Simoza was in Latin America months before.

The headmaster told Rosario early the next morning when he was notified by the Suretee. He asked the boy if he wanted to return home, telling him plainly that the nature of the crime was such that there was little or nothing remaining of his parents to be respectfully buried.

He declined, electing instead to complete his studies uninterrupted for the year. His mother's parents were now also departed, and there was no other family for him to draw upon. It was time to stand fully on his own two feet, alone, and move forward for his own sake. He had already been raised to do so and now was the beginning of his self-responsibility. He felt more than ready and stood certainly able and willing to go it alone. Rosario had been a young boy long enough; manhood emerged.

CHAPTER TWO

The Man-Child Comes of Age

The boy moved on with life without remorse. No other choices existed for safe harbor to comfort him. He stuck to his studies, his outdoor routines, and mostly kept to himself. He sailed easily through the last three years of school in two years and went to college at the Sorbonne for premedicine. After continued accelerated studies, he completed college and medical school by twenty-five. By age twenty-seven, he completed a medical residency in surgery and trauma with an emergency room background. Now he was ready to join society to apply his medical skills.

Rosario had no need to garner money and no desire to apply his skills simply to earn a living for one day after the next. Moreover, his solitary and feral nature mandated that he depart from the course of those he had seen before him leaving for private practice. He wanted something different and fuller.

His grandparents had left his mother well-heeled with more ten million dollars, which yielded well over a million dollars a year after taxes with the investments of her trust; he could hardly spend that. Except to smooth the way, he had no real use for the money, and it just kept accumulating.

His needs were simple, and he lived without any real expenses. His luxuries were zero. He drove a modest red Morris Mini minor convertible and lived in rented rooms on Rue Street near the Postal Bar across from the vast main post office complex.

His only real expense was women, but not in the traditional manner. As a younger man with money, even in boarding school in Zurich, he had shown no interest in school girls. He had been advanced for years in dealing with adults, and teenagers held no interest for him. He enjoyed adult women, and they were to be found freely within the society of fallen women. He took his pleasures and comforts there and changed not at all when he became a young doctor. He had no interest in courting or marrying well. No one was present to introduce him into the elite circles of debutantes. He resisted any need to develop such beneficial relationships, even when offered a casual opportunity by one of his classmates or professors suggesting their own family members or friends. Simply put, he preferred the company of whores and found them much more attractive. It was a lottery he could well afford and did. In many ways, he found them more honest than the women of his age who were husband-gathering or trading up after already being married.

Likewise, since he had never lost his thirst for revenge for his parents' murders, he wished no emotional attachments to hold him back. Revenge remained a subcurrent of his development, but it was difficult to reconcile with his pledge to save lives rather than to take them. Nevertheless, he did not want to become adjusted to circumstances that would altogether destroy his murderous revenge fantasies by conventional marriage, fatherhood, and a staid professional lifestyle. That left him few practical choices as to his life course.

His need for action and his unconventional behavior limited his career path, especially in France. They narrowed his field of selection. They did not, however, defeat his goal of overall freedom while practicing his art of medicine. Rather, they strengthened his ultimate decision to practice medicine within the ranks of the French Foreign Legion. He entered the legion at the accelerated rank of captain and practiced his healing within the corps, getting posted to various legion military bases throughout France, its territories, and established posts.

The French Foreign Legion he knew was no picnic. It was rough living with long hours in difficult circumstances, often in makeshift hospitals and surgeries. The nurses were enlisted men and so were virtually all patients. Officers usually returned to France for private civil medical care. Thus, his patients were the rough-and-ready young enlisted men of suspicious but forgiven background. No one asked about their pasts; it was not a topic for discussion. Given his own private feelings, he fit readily with their membership and enjoyed its camaraderie, socializing at will with officers and enlisted men alike.

Many enlisted men were accomplished murderers and criminals of every sort but with all sins forgiven and one step into a new, protected identity. That applied to him too. His prints were expunged in France, even within the medical society records, and he was provided with a new identity, finally being named Rosario. It was a new beginning with a strange name for an orphaned Jewish boy. Yet the identity fit him, and soon, he grew into it.

The lower ranks of the legion were populated by hard men. He treated as many knife and gun wounds from brawls as he did wounds from actual military adventures. He quickly observed that, after the first two years of an initial six-year enlistment, 90 percent of the men had lost a quarter or more of their teeth from infighting and had incurred repeated knife wounds and broken bones. By the end of the first tour, most were badly scarred and had few teeth. None failed to suffer some type of permanent injury.

This was the group of men he came to enjoy and with whom he prospered in his own relationships. To say they were bonded was a gross denial of the full strength of their esprit de corps. As a group, they merged into one unit—"One for all, and all for one! Mess with one dog, and the pack would be on you. These hard men became friends forever. He needed only to summon them. There were no holds barred.

Few comrades sought to brawl with him. He was revered by his fellow troopers, and they needed him to heal them too regularly to risk his enmity. In his own way, he became a shining star. He would do anything to help these men survive, and they did the same for him. It was a mutual bank account to be drawn upon or repaid at any time or in any place. It would be soon enough that he would draw upon it as he walked the Natchez Trace, bound for Louisiana during his sabbatical following the end of his first enlistment before starting his next with Major Oakleafs.

Virtually every army in the world kept its medics, doctors, and nurses from active military action. They were not trained for military action, rather they were just there to heal. Not so in the legion. The doctors, including Rosario, were fully trained, and their deployment included active military duty with full assault and weapons training. They were also involved in the killing process. For Rosario, there was no problem reconciling his medicine with the need to be an effective soldier. It was consistent with his desire for revenge. In his first tour of duty, he was involved in at least six firefights from Anguilla to Sudan. He had killed rather than be killed.

In further development of his military skills, Rosario applied for service in the most elite division of the legion: the airborne corps. That corps was for their best and brightest. He learned to jump, gun in hand, and joined the elite legion delta forces, ready to kill or heal as the case might be. He had earned his jump wings and the camaraderie of the men he jumped with and served. By tour's end, he had nine assault jumps under his belt and at least four verified kills. He had saved dozens of lives and had never been wounded or injured jumping so far.

CHAPTER THREE

The Arrest

The Mississippi sun rises early in Southern autumn. By five thirty a.m., it was knocking at Rosario's eyelids, forcing him awake and banning any further sleep. The birds had long since been up.

He was living rough with no shower or shave. It was simply "up and at 'em," "rise and shine." He would pack his blanket, drink his cold takeaway coffee from last night, and then be on down the road. After years of cutting and sewing legionnaires at all times of the night, his body had adjusted to irregular meals and routines of work and rest. It kept him active, alert, and on his toes. His mind had learned to come awake quickly from a dead start, and that day was no exception. Before he was fully erect, he was wide awake and aware of his environment.

He drank the cold, strong coffee down and awaited its jolt of energy. His studies in medicine had taught him that it would take a good quarter of an hour for the caffeine to jolt him, but physically he thought it there already with anticipation. It had a placebo effect on him, bringing him around as though the effect was already fully on him. He enjoyed the slightly stale, cold, strong taste of the leftover brew. It was what he was used to from the barracks at home in France along with the smell and company of hard men, his own manner of friends.

Alone but not lonely, he lifted his backpack and left the woodside clearing adjoining the road. His legs warmed up to his hiking pace. He caught the early warmth of the still rising sun as it played peekaboo among the yet unturned leaves of tall trees; they covered its full glare and soon-to-be full, warming rays. Morning had always been his favorite time of day. It was clean, new, and fresh with a promise of things to come, even if he had been up all night triaging wounded soldiers or just caring for the lingering sick ones.

Keeping to the trace, Rosario bypassed Jackson on the east by a good ten miles. Jackson had no modern beltway, because Mississippi remained one of the poorest states, with its capitol city one of the smallest in the Union if not the actual top winner for the prize of least developed. There was and had never been any real money for developing roadways, because welfare and hospital growth had taken up all of the financial slack in the budget. The economy was just plain staying alive for its citizens. No public works existed for fun or the entertainment of the population. Thus roads were left to be, except as the prison gangs cleaned and repaired them.

Most people blew through Mississippi without stopping, using the federally funded interstates to reach Florida, Louisiana, or Texas. Their money did not come to rest in Mississippi. Indeed, Rosario thought even he was just passing through. His real terminus was at the bayous and their Creole culture. He had no intention of frolic and detour among the Southern white Baptist Klan-loving, Jew-baiting, Mississippi Dixie-crats who had never fully recovered from their backlash to radical reconstruction a century and a half before, after the Civil War. He knew all strangers were suspect, since the death of the three civil rights workers Schwerner, Chaney, and Goodman at the hands of the police in Neshoba Country during the civil rights voter registration movements in the early 1960s.

On the other hand, he believed that the natural beauty of Mississippi was nested in the state's forests and wildlife and that autumn was its best time of year. For this reason, he was walking south through it in full bloom instead of coming north from the New Orleans delta into the more northern Louisiana parishes. The march itself was six of one or a half dozen of the other, so he had chosen beauty over the perhaps more direct route. He would come to regret it, never knowing in advance the price he was to pay for the toll of passage.

Midday came and went, but Rosario did not quit his pace, projecting thirty miles to hike each day, landing him at his target area on the evening of the third day or on the morning thereafter. He was never to make it!

Twenty-five to thirty miles below Jackson, as the sun played late-day hide and seek, he saw a police cruiser blow by him north at eighty miles per hour or more. Its approach was easily heard. Rosario had kept to the leftmost blacktopped part of the oncoming lane and had no concern for the few trucks and occasional cars that had passed him during the day, never stopping or acknowledging him in any way, not even slowing their excessive speeds.

Less than two minutes after he was passed, Rosario spotted a car approaching from the south and knew by sound that it was the same police car. Instinct told him to leave the road and seek cover in the woods, moving on through them undetected as he could easily do. He knew the men would never follow him in deeply, soon giving up and returning to the comfort of their air conditioning. He rejected his thoughts initially as irrational. Even if it was the same police car, he had done nothing wrong. He was not a vagrant Rambo but a well-documented foreign traveler, simply enjoying a nature hike. He had no reason for concern and expected the car to simply pass him yet again.

He knew he was wrong. He could see the car slowing and its hood moved downward, reacting to the decrease in speed, catching the sun as it did. The car stopped abreast of him, and the darkened passenger window came down.

"Good day, son. Out for a late-day walk?" The question was what Rosario expected for an opener. The man was not. Rosario was surprised by the "son," not sure that the trooper was older. Maybe it was Southern or police liberty, he thought, spoken to make him passive or submissive to authority.

"Yes, sir. Just on my way going south."

"Where do you live, boy?" came the reply.

Rosario was taken aback. He had not been called "boy" since boarding school and hardly then and not successfully. After all, he had been the man-child. He realized it was a police technique, so his choices were to rebel or take it in stride and let it pass, see what happened if he used sugar and not salt, play the word game. He kept it short.

"I'm traveling."

"That I can see, but from where to where is what I want to hear, stranger."

"I came into Jackson Airport yesterday, and I'm hiking south to Louisiana on the trace." True was true Rosario thought, and he saw no problem letting it out.

"Where were you last night, boy?" There it was rising up again. Rosario decided to up the ante a bit and see where it was all going.

"Asleep."

"Well, now, 'where' was the question, not 'what.' Asleep where?"

"In the woods."

"What woods?"

"Where? I figure maybe eight miles south of the airport in the trace."

"How far from the church did you get, boy?"

Rosario remembered the church on a hill he had passed. It had been so pretty in stark white, glowing in the coming darkness and framed by the sun.

"Probably an hour's walk south before I stopped at the diner for dinner and bedded down not far from there."

The driver exited. He leaned over the hood, gun in hand.

"Put down the backpack, boy. Step back from it, tuck your hands in the front of your pants below the waist, and do not move."

As he spoke, the officer in the passenger seat opened his door and moved swiftly around to the rear deck, drawing his weapon and taking cover behind the troop vehicle. The two cops were both aiming down on him in less than three seconds. That was not what he had expected in the "land of the free and the home of the brave." This was no routine stop. Something foul was afoot, and he was the quarry. "Shit happens" and it was happening now. The flow of peaceful conversation was interrupted and over. They were down to the bottom line. The time to take stock of the situation was over, and so was his chance for bolting into the woods.

"Ollie is just fooling with you, youngster, putting you through the process, to see how you take it, see you react," said the driver cop. He was older looking. Wrinkled worry lines marked his face.

"I'm not playing like, Ollie. We've been up half the night and all day finding you. I knew you were the one soon as I heard what you did and where you were seen, stranger. Now I'm tired and angry. I'm ready to wrap this up and get on home. Any shit out of you, and I do it the easy way and drop you. Get it right the first time. 'cause I ain't Ollie, and I'm not fooling around. Just say 'yes' so I know you got it. Nothing more."

"Yes," Rosario said, thinking about what his real choices were, if he had any other than just going with the drift.

"You left-handed or right?"

"Right-handed."

"Put your right leg out front and kneel on your left knee on the ground. Keep your hands in your pants, and do it slow, boy."

Rosario complied, understanding that the older cop was no fool. He was putting him off balance so he could not lash out.

"Good. Ollie, throw him your cuffs."

Ollie pitched them quickly, and they landed in front of Rosario maybe eight inches to the right of his grounded legs. Obviously, these cops had been through this routine many times before. Ollie was ready the second the boss told him to act.

"Now remove your right hand slowly—I mean, slowly—and pick up the cuffs."

Rosario did so, wondering if they were smart enough to cuff him behind the back or leave his hands out in front.

"Let your left hand out slowly and cuff your right tightly so it hits the skin all around. Do not stand up or you get shot. Now we're down to it. If you want to be brave and think you can make it, now's the time to try, because after this, you're all done up, and we are on our way home. Otherwise, give it up and stop scamming and do what you're told."

The man was moving down the driver's door past the rear deck out to ten feet perpendicular to Rosario's left side. He was positioned to shoot him clear in the side. Ollie was also moving around the front of the car past his right side behind him.

"Bring your right hand behind you." Ollie stepped in close behind.

"Ollie is going to cuff you, so bring your left hand behind you slowly, and do not stand or I'll shoot you in the legs. Got it?"

"Yes." Rosario felt Ollie take the open cuff and flick it closed over his left wrist, clamping it down to make sure it was tight. He reached in to squeeze out any room that was left over in the right cuff.

"Now we are done."

"Move him, Ollie."

Ollie hoisted him up, pulling from behind on the middle of the handcuff chain. He was none too polite as he pushed Rosario toward the rear of the cruiser, where the door was already being opened. The older cop took over guiding him in, so Ollie didn't thump his head on the doorjamb as Rosario thought he would.

"We want you home in one piece if we can, with no spoil spots making up your pretty face, boy. Now shut up, behave yourself, and we will have you at your new home soon enough. I don't want to have to stop to teach you manners on the way in, but I will if you act up."

Rosario knew now something big was afoot, and he was the target, the one to blame, the scapegoat.

"What did I do?"

"Shut up, stranger. I told you once. You know as well as I, so don't play possum. I know a stone-cold killer when I see one, and you're it, boy. You're the one, all right. Don't try putting a game on me. Anymore out of you and you're coming in looking like spoiled banana skin."

The back door slammed, and he was already locked in and caged by the mesh rising from the front seat headrests to the ceiling. No rear door lock levers existed for him to try to make it out.

Ollie moved over to Rosario's backpack. He opened it and turned it upside down, watching the blanket and toiletries fall down. His passport came out last. Ollie picked it alone up and handed it to the driver, who thumbed through it.

"You're a long way from home, frog," he said. "Going to be a long time before you see Paris again, son, even if they don't hang you just for being a foreigner."

He and Ollie took their seats, and off they went, literally hightailing it down the highway, sirens blazing. It took a good half hour to reach the downtown Jackson municipal jail. The cruiser pulled up under a covered, walled port at the rear entrance, like the cops were bringing in Oswald, just like Dallas before Jack Ruby laid him out from coast to coast on live national TV.

There were no reporters lurking, but when the car stopped a half-dozen SWAT-uniformed, oversize officers formed a semicircle around the right rear door as it clicked open. A half-dozen strong hands pulled Rosario up and out, not letting him fall as he otherwise would have. An orange front-and-back, thigh-long bulletproof vest was dropped over him, making him resemble a depression street salesman adorned with placards on both sides.

Out of nowhere came a wheelchair-like device that resembled an electric chair. He was thrust into it, and his legs were clamped down. He heard the electric jail doors unbolt. Then he was wheeled inside, still surrounded by his six-man SWAT detail, which was now at rest. The men were joking about him, knowing their job had been done without incident.

There were still no photographers as he entered a large pock-marked, poorly painted, and penned receiving area with benches on three sides that were made of wooden slats. The benches had foot chains and arm restraint loops of steel every four feet. It was a poor man's transport holding area, and it smelled of human distress, sweat, and urine. The gate slammed closed behind him. Another bolted door clicked open, rolling halfway back. To the right was a small, enclosed, Plexiglas sully port with switches for the doors. It held two officers.

A heavyset man in a white shirt, gold braids, and a gold badge stepped up. His badge said, "Chief, Jackson, Mississippi." With him were two very large officers who were dressed in blues. They unlocked his restraints and pulled him up from either side. The chief stood, looking him up and down and saying nothing. His face full of disgust; he looked pale and sick to his stomach.

"Book him for murder, clean him up, dress him in orange, and let me know when he is ready. No food just coffee. The judge is waiting on him, and I don't want him hurling in the courtroom like what happened two weeks ago. Just coffee. Print him after he is arraigned, because no bail is going to be set.

"Mister, my road boys told me your passport says you are French. That's your business. I am going to give you our Miranda warning." He pulled a small card from his breast pocket. "Do you speak and write English?"

"Yes, sir," Rosario said as though he was talking to his own superior officers.

"Good. Let's get on with it."

The chief read the full card, muttering the warning and Rosario's right to counsel in a steady emotionless voice just like in a TV program. Almost like a magician, the guard to his left produced in a practiced manner a sheet of paper with the warnings printed on them. He handed it with a deft move to the chief, who reached out for it without looking, knowing it was there. It was a practiced act, almost like a football game halftime show.

"Read it and sign it, or tell me now if you don't understand it, mister. You should know we are being taped and recorded, so now is the time."

"Yes, sir," Rosario said, knowing they would have to uncuff him.

"Mister, we are going to uncuff you so you can read it and sign it. For all I know, you are a one-man killing machine with your arms and legs. It won't matter. You can't leave here unless the doors open, and they won't. Both my men are former marine special forces and here to take good care of me. I bet on the two of them, so forget about it if you have something stupid in mind."

Not wanting for a reply, the officers moved behind him on either side, taking out what Rosario knew were fifty thousand-volt tasers from their Sam Brown equipment belts. Gently, but unlike before, the man on the right unlocked his cuffs, taking them away. The chief saw that Rosario's wrists were red from the binding, especially because he had stayed cuffed in the back in the troop car. He had had to pull his arms away while he sat against them with pressure from the rear seat from speeding down the highway.

"Get him some salve for his wrists, and make sure he is front-cuffed next time with a ring belt. Tell the boys upstairs he gets a real calm shower and shave with no water hose bullshit. If he falls in the shower or gets tuned up behind my back, tell them they will be picking cotton, and I will know because this man will tell me," he said. "Please read and sign this. If you will, because you are foreign, I would ask you to read it out loud so we all know you can."

Rosario read, signed off, and was led inside. The chief disappeared, and he entered the lock up. It was to be a long stay.

CHAPTER FOUR

The Arraignment

The sun was nearly all the way down before they moved Rosario from the municipal jail's third floor pass to the Jackson City court on the same level in the municipal building. It was a pathway designed to avoid elevators and citizens when the sheriff's officers moved high-profile prisoners for arraignment or trial. They could also clear the area in advance and seal the floor, keeping both the accused and the court safer. That day, they had cleared the reporters, who knew the court was extraordinarily into extra hours.

Rosario was cleaned, dressed in orange prison clothes, and chained hand and foot, which made him shuffle forward rather than move normally and forced him to do the perp walk for those present, most of whom were court personnel. Even the secretaries and inner-office staff members of the other judges had turned out for the event.

He was guided by the sheriff into courtroom number one before the presiding judge, the Honorable R. Homer Barrett Jr, PJMC. As he passed through the leather, swinging, ten-foot entrance doors he heard the familiar *bang* of the court's gavel and the bailiff's cry.

"Court in session. The Honorable R. Homer Barrett Jr, presiding judge. Be seated. No talking. All phones or recording devices are to be shut off."

The large room was nearly full. The judge's staff scurried about, looking busy but with nothing happening, knowing they were in for a good show and some real overtime; they were already about two hours past their normal day's end.

"Call the calendar," the Court said. The judge was already present and seated on his oak judicial throne, breaking away from banter with his staff and visitors—holding court of his own, awaiting his prisoner.

"State versus Rosario Baloute, your honor."

Rosario remained standing; he had not been offered a seat by the court officers, who had already taken over control of him from the transporting sheriffs, both of whom stood behind him, ready to act if need be. The court officers stood in front and slightly to either side of Rosario, facing him.

"Is the defendant represented by counsel?" the Court asked knowing the answer full well but protecting the record of the proceedings.

"Hearing no reply, the court appoints counsel for the defendant. Present attorney Wilber Armstrong, Esq., of the distinguished office of the public defender of Jackson, Mississippi."

"Wilber Armstrong, your honor. Counsel for the defendant of Jackson, Mississippi," the petite, suited man said. He was standing off to Rosario's right and neither approached him nor otherwise acknowledged his presence.

"That's what I like about you, Wilber. You always speak right up when needed, doing your part for our fine system of justice. Let me assure the defendant of your good counsel and the court's satisfaction in your appearance on his behalf in these proceedings."

"Normally, I tell you, Mr. Baloute, that you would have time to consult with counsel before moving forward with a plea disposition. However, today, that is not necessary. You are charged with the ritualistic, sadistic murder of three people. Because these are capital offenses, the court must enter a plea of not guilty for you at this stage, pending further proceedings. Standing at counsel table to your left is the state's attorney Buheul Staggers, Esq. He is not a Jackson City attorney as might be normal in lesser matters but rather a distinguished member of the Office of the Attorney General of the State of Mississippi. He is the first assistant chief of the criminal division. As it may choose, the attorney general's office can enter statewide to prosecute certain matters. They have so elected to prosecute your matter. Do you understand, Mr. Baloute?"

"Yes, your honor."

"'That is your name, is it not? It was written on your passport, and I am told that the picture was yours. You are a French citizen recently arrived in our area. Is that all accurate, sir?"

"Yes, your honor."

"Do you read and write and speak English?"

"Yes, judge."

"Do you understand the nature of these proceedings, where you are, what is going on here?"

"Yes."

"Do you have private counsel present or whom you would like to summon, pending an adjournment?"

"Not on hand, judge."

"Good. Then we will proceed. You have been arrested and charged this afternoon with the crime of murder within the city of Jackson, Mississippi, of three citizens of our state. How do you plead, Mr. Armstrong, on this defendant's behalf?"

"Not guilty, your honor, may it please the court."

"Nothing pleases me in capital cases, Mr. Armstrong. Let it be known. I accept your plea. Do you waive the reading of the charges? Bailiff, hand Wilber the complaint. Take time to look at it, counsel," said the judge as the bailiff placed the typed form green pages on the defendant's counsel table.

Taking them up and turning them rapidly one after the other, Armstrong spoke out without comment to Rosario.

"Waive the reading, your honor."

Everybody knew the cat was already out of the bag (three murders!) and there was no sense dealing with the sordid details in the late-day session, reading out the crimes for ten long minutes. The charging papers had covered in all. Everybody but Rosario knew the story, so why bother ... better to get on with it.

"Will the court set bail, your honor?"

"Normally, Mr. Armstrong, I would let you argue that and hear from the state, but there is no need for ceremony. The crimes stated are of the highest order: violent and unredeeming as to the victims. The defendant has no roots in the community and is a foreign national. I find that there is a greatly enhanced risk of flight. His background and prior involvement with the legal system is yet unknown. I am not inclined, at this time, to consider or grant bail. Now I will hear you, if you want. You can sit down, Mr. Staggers, Esq. I know you will oppose bail, including based on the criteria this court has already set forth. I have no need to hear from you."

"Nothing further, your honor," said Wilber Armstrong, again not even closing ranks with Rosario to learn if he had any input or inquiries before the court session shut down.

"Bail denied. Remand the prisoner to the county jail, maximum security tier. These proceedings are closed. The public is to remain seated while the officers remove the prisoner until my bailiff advises that you may rise and leave. No exceptions. Have a good evening, one and all." The judge rose and stepped down from behind his elevated desk, leaving through a door to his chambers.

Rosario was removed. There was no discussion with, Mr. Armstrong.

CHAPTER FIVE

In Between

Rosario was removed to the outskirts of Jackson, down near the river, to what appeared to be one of the most modern structures in the otherwise historic, antebellum-structured city, which favored architecture of more than a hundred years old. The exception was a few newer hotels from the '50s and '60s and hospital complexes with adjacent staff apartments that bordered the highway to Canton with its fast food and outlet chains. The remainder was Old South, in contrast to the jail's modern state-of-the-art orange brick with an overabundance of razor wire and at least a dozen armed guard towers.

Rosario was housed alone in the maximum lockdown area for twenty-three hours a day. He had no contact with other inmates, and he was fed in his cell. One hour a day, he could come out to shower and walk in a walled holding area outside that was twenty by forty feet. There were no gym, basketball, card games, or smoking it up with the other prisoners for him. He had no television, radio, or even the Bible. The library book cart did not reach him, and no chaplain ministered to his needs. He might as well have already been convicted.

On the middle of the second afternoon, Wilber Armstrong showed up, being mustered in by two jailers. One carried a folding metal chair that was placed outside the cell. This was as far as Mr. Armstrong was allowed. They would not be using the attorney conference rooms to plot and plan.

"Press the door buzzer over here on the back entrance wall when you are ready to leave, counselor. We will come get you. The doors will not open for you automatically. If you are still here at five p.m., the tour changes, and we do the count. There is a lockdown during dinner. You will have to wait to be buzzed out until nearly six if you are running late. Best to get out early if you can."

"It won't be long, officer. That's still two hours off, and I should be done well before that. Thank you for the heads-up. See you soon. Will you two be back for me?"

"As long as our tour is not up and there are no other problems. Don't wait too close to five p.m. or you're stuck."

Off they went, disappearing as Armstrong seated himself. He had a small briefcase that looked like a leather envelope with a zipper and two pull-out handles but he reached for no papers.

"You're somewhat of a mystery, Mr. Baloute. I was waiting for your prints and reports to come back. The state attorney contacted Interpol. Normally, he would not share anything with me, but since nothing came back, he was surprised and wanted me to know. He wants me to drag it out of you, I suppose. All we know is you are a French national, your name, your date of birth, your height, your eye color, and your home city: Marseilles. Interpol was able to provide no other information about your background, schooling, or work. You exist, but yet you do not—no car, no wife, no military or birth history, no school record, no medical records in a socialized treatment country. Let me tell you, with all our freedoms in the good ole US of A, you couldn't stay below the radar like that here. Who are you?"

"I am who I am, counselor. Let's leave it at that for now. Maybe later, maybe not."

"Did you kill them, Mr. Baloute?"

"No."

"Are you sure?"

"Yes."

"I've been doing this for a while, defending people. Some did it; some did not. Some admitted it; most did not. The conviction rate is pretty high here, especially in big crime, high-profile cases. I'm told they have witnesses who put you at the scene, finger you. Whether you did it or not, there is a big chance of conviction. If you did, tell me, and let me see if I can work a deal. The attorney general has a lot of influence.

"They convict even the innocent. It plays well with the public—convictions—gets you re-elected. Lose cases, especially big ones, and it's back to starting private practice again after you have been gone for a while. Plus you're a loser; no firms want you. You are barred from handling defense matters for five years, to avoid influence with your former colleagues. It's down to divorces and slip-and-fall cases, if you can even get that type of work. So convictions, good or bad, are the order of the day. Don't kid yourself. To get their conviction, they will bend the rules, upset the cart of justice, pervert the law. Better to save your skin, if you can. Admit guilt and make your best deal."

"No, thank you. I did not murder anyone. No guilt. No plea. If I did it, I would tell you. I have no idea of who was killed, where, or why. I'm not their boy or yours either, Mr. Armstrong."

"Here is what we do, mister. You plead guilty, and I'll get you temporary insanity. They insulted you, injured your pride. You went crazy, and soon, it was all over. You'll do only a few years and not in a jail. Get you to the state asylum. They got women there too. Soon you'll be out and on your way home to France with no one chasing you. That's the best deal you'll get, especially if they seek the death penalty. That's usually why the state's attorney general takes over. This was a bad crime with lots of publicity. Folks liked these people, especially the two children. You're not going to get off easy, even if you didn't do it. You're a stranger. You're out of water here. Local people's word over yours. What do you say?"

"No."

"Think it over. Don't be so quick. You're in big trouble here. No other way out. Admit your guilt, and take your medicine. A smaller dose is better than the full load. Time to smarten up, learn how things work here."

Who do you work for, Mr. Lawyer Armstrong? I told you I didn't do it. You've got the wrong boy. Not me. When do you start representing me? Find out the truth. Investigate the facts, and get to the defense."

"I don't do that kind of work. I don't try cases. I'm no good at the trial section. Other public defenders do that. I'll send them over, but you will see I'm right. Later on, you'll know you needed to listen. It will be too late then. You'll find out."

"Send them over. It's time to get started, gather up the evidence, knit together the defense, help prove me innocent."

"Have a good day, mister. No sense in my staying longer."

Armstrong stood, leaving his chair in place, and strode to the buzzer. He leaned on it for a good while, knowing that, with less than that, they would keep him waiting. Ten seconds sounded like trouble, and they came at once. It always worked. After all, he was still a government lawyer. No jailer wanted him getting hurt on his watch.

Less than a minute later, the same twosome appeared, keyed open the barred door, and let him out. Off he went without so much as a nod, like a tiny Santa after the toys had been laid out by the chimney. He was gone in a flash.

CHAPTER SIX
Trial

The state did not seek the death penalty. Due to the spontaneous nature of the crimes, it would be impossible to convince even a Mississippi jury that a Frenchman flew into Jackson and premeditatedly killed three people he had never known, two of whom were children, that same afternoon. It was too hard a sale even for their prosecutorial talents. If it didn't fly (and they knew it wouldn't), then Rosario would walk, and they would be out looking for another job in the private sector.

Because Mississippi was one of the poorest states, private lawyering paid far less than state work did. The private sector also had no real perks like so many days off, state insurance, state cars, the gold badge, the gun, and everyone calling you "sir." It was far better to convict him of a lower-grade crime of nonpremeditated homicide than to risk his beating the conviction.

They also knew that the real problem with a fuller conviction would be the court. In Jackson, only one judge heard homicide matters: the Honorable Reginald Stittin. The problem was that he was a Yankee, a New York City–raised and trained Columbia Law School scholar.

He had come to Mississippi an army colonel posted to the base JAG Division. He was still a young but lucky boy, and he met and married Mary Beth Cruthers, whose old marine family went back to the Civil War days.

They owned some of the largest tobacco and catfish farms in the state. Because he was really wealthy, the judge ran the matters of his court just as he chose; there was no manipulating him. He had authored the state criminal law treatises and lectured on them at Mississippi State School of Law gratis. He was a homicide authority. He gave people a fair shake. If they tried to shoot the moon on this one, Rosario would be home free. There was no sense even trying.

Rosario got the good news of his diminished trial setting from Taylor Hawkins, Esq., a public defender in the criminal trial section. He was young too, a little over thirty. He had defended murderers before, but mostly he had defended disenfranchised welfare youths who had killed over drugs, women, or bar fights.

All cases were invariably heard by white jurors, since few black juror candidates made it into the jury pool. If they were chosen, either side excused them until no more were left.

Hawkins had been helped in his prior work by a long-standing white Mississippi jury joke, which was actually reflected in his trial outcomes as a practical matter. He called them "wins." The thought was that, if a black man killed another black man, then the jury would go easy on him so he could be released quicker in the hopes that he would do it again. Hawkins never had a case in which a black man had killed a white citizen. But he knew the score from history and the matters of others. Such a defendant would get the book thrown at him and not in jail or by visiting "sparky," the state's electric chair. In the not so long ago days, he would have simply been lynched.

Almost every state, Mississippi included, recognizes the right of a defendant in any criminal matter to have a speedy trial, usually within six months after arrest and charging. When it suited them, the state moved the case more quickly, and Judge Stittin would comply, assuming the defense agreed it was ready or had no other pretrial discovery or investigation issues. So it was that, only six weeks later, Rosario was in court with his trial ready to move.

Hawkins had seen him a few times and listened to his story about arriving, hiking, eating, and bedding down in the woods. Rosario recalled his passing the church—the crime scene itself. By his description of the lowering sun, the crime had probably not already occurred, but it was a close call because autopsies had a two-hour window. That alone was enough to place him at the scene. Hawkins couldn't say he could not have done it in the time allowed, because he was walking. There was no way to prove how much time had been taken up. There was no timeline to help him. He could have hitched a ride part of the way from the airport. Besides, how long does it take a lunatic to kill and string up two children and a frail adult, if he was in wiry, strong condition like Rosario? Carving the crosses on their chests while they hung and their blood dripped into the already reddish Mississippi dirt would not have been a long process. The absence of forensic proof—no blood on his person or clothes—was not a defense. He had had nearly a full day to clean up before his arrest.

Hawkins had spoken to the people at the diner. No one seemed to remember him, even though he was there for an hour at least and left with coffee. Most diner workers would remember a stranger, especially a hiker. Hawkins though it was peculiar that none of the workers spoke up. It would have verified Rosario's story but not provided a defense to the murders, which were likely done before Rosario stopped in to eat.

However, Hawkins was sure that Rosario had been there, because he was able to describe the outside and the inner design of the diner in full detail. He even gave a pretty good description of his waitress, but he had no name for her, because the diner girls wore no name pins. They were also generic bottle blonds who were overweight and quick speaking with bad skin; they showed as much cleavage in their black uniforms as a female Vegas blackjack dealer. All people really saw was their pad as they took an order.

Rosario knew the New York post office had the famous inscription "Neither rain nor snow or gloom of night." He thought that Mississippi courthouses should be similarly inscribed. In Mississippi, there would be "quick trials and quick convictions." Six weeks to trial was only 25 percent of the Speedy Trial Act—period. How could you be ready to protect someone's life in a quarter of the time? His life at that, too! He knew he was on a ride on a train with no brakes.

So far, they hadn't even questioned him about his background or training as a doctor. He was a person who saved lives. On the other hand, he could not deny his military background and that he had killed before, albeit during military conflict. Nevertheless, it made him a killer and to the small-minded a person whose disposition was likely bent to kill, even perhaps like it or miss it. They would think his mind was already around some corner of insanity, that he was a person who killed and was accustomed to killing. Testifying would open up his background, and it was best to leave it alone and make them prove it. The jury would know he had entered a plea of not guilty.

Nevertheless, he believed that Hawkins and his investigators were not doing their job. They should be out using their time and resources to find out who had done it. It seemed that little or no energy was going in that direction. At best, they were focused on damage control, which was not likely to save his bacon. It was hardly proactive. It left him exposed like a nerve on a tooth taking in air. It gave him no chance to have the charges dismissed. He would be brought to trial in a short time without any really effective defense or evidence.

An all-white, all-male jury was selected in less than two hours. No women or blacks were even in the two jury panels that were called. The voir dire was directed by the court and mostly limited to disclosing prejudice about foreigners or one's ability to hear the sordid details of murder most foul.

During the trial, the dead woman's husband, Minister Caulfield, described returning home to his small church to find his wife and the two children hanging from the long limbs of a sturdy oak tree only fifteen feet to the right of the church entrance. They were trussed up with a knotted clothesline with shirts open, showing their newly carved crosses. Each cross was about five inches long, and the top bar was just slightly shorter. The top cut was crooked on all three, descending slightly from left to right as though cut by a leftie. The minister made no such observations, but the forensic pictures of the crime scene showed it in the standard impersonal, up-close photos of death taken while the victims were hanging. It was motivational evidence, properly admitted but just as likely to anger and inflame the jury.

The children were seven-year-old twins, a boy and a girl named Jacob and Judith Wells. Their mother was a parishioner, but the minister's wife cared for them just as they had begun kindergarten until their mother could retrieve them after work, which was usually by six p.m. On the day of the murders, she arrived after the minister but before the police. She saw them while they were still hanging, waiting for the photo detail and the coroner.

At trial, the minister set it all out the best for the both of them as survivors, trying to spare her the need to also testify. When asked about his wife, he blurted out that he would never get the sight of them out of his mind and he knew Mrs. Wells wouldn't either. No one moved to strike his prejudicial comments or for curative instruction. It would not have helped. It would not have overcome the pictures of the dead, carved bodies with stretched necks. It would likely only upset the jurors even more, because it was so true. They weren't likely to forget the crime scene for the rest of time either.

The coroner was a quick, practical witness. In his unbroken chain of evidence, He spoke of his work at the homicide scene and the ensuing transport of the dead. He noted his overall gross findings of autopsied body parts. He pronounced the cause of death for each victim as strangulation, noting that the carvings and hangings were postmortem. He opined that the killer may have been left-handed but that there was no way to be sure. He believed that the killings were somehow anti-Christian and ritualistic. His attempt at prejudicial testimony was stricken, because he was a pathologist and not a psychiatrist. The jury did not need his say-so to believe it was the handiwork of a sick-minded anti-Christ. Common sense and pictures of the crime scene were all the jurors needed.

Mrs. Wells was still called briefly. Judge Stittin limited her testimony to how and why the children were at the church. She was barred from speaking about seeing her dead children. It would duplicate the minister's observations. The crime scene forensic photos made the jury upset enough.

The Stittin court was not allowing reversible error. This case in his court would go in clean enough. The defendant would not get off on appeal because Judge Stittin allowed trial error to occur. He had ruled over dozens of homicide cases, and he knew where the lines in the sands of error were. They wouldn't cross them. Quick trials and quick convictions could happen perhaps, but not reversible error. Perish the thought—not in his court for sure.

There was little cross-examination by Public Defender Hawkins. The witnesses were relating details to which there could be no reply. Even Rosario had to concede, by his own recollection, that when he passed the church, no bodies were hanging and so he was at the crime scene before the episode. He could be of no help in advancing any evidence on his own behalf for Hawkins to use with the state's witnesses.

The coroner also testified that the stranglings had occurred inside the church, based on luminal tracings of saliva from all three victims in the rear rectory area. Postmortem, the killer had trussed up the victims with clothesline in the church and then hung each one, risking exposure. To hang them and then carve them, he had stood on a relocated picnic bench, which had been left nearby bloodstained. No traces of foot size or clues as to any vehicle used had been present. This further condemned Rosario, because he was carless and afoot. No fingerprints of Rosario's were recovered. Any that were detected were those of church members or the victims or were just unknown.

Then came the trump card witness: a waitress who had just been located. She was a fill-in waitress that night, a substitute who had worked that night and not for months before. She was not on the weekly roster and had been paid in cash for one night's work. A repeat visit to the diner to prepare possible rebuttal witnesses with new question had led to her discovery a day after the trial started ... so said the state. On the late morning of the third trial day (being the first trial session after the waitress' discovery), the state provided the defense counsel, Hawkins, with her statement. She was called as a witness minutes thereafter.

There was little or nothing Hawkins could do about it. He was not surprised by the eleventh-hour discovery. It happened from time to time, and he had the basis to assure the court that an adjournment would lead to his uncovering rebuttal evidence. Hawkins knew seconds after he studied her statement that her testimony would convict Rosario, even if it was circumstantial and her word alone. He asked Rosario if he recognized her, but with the passage of time, Rosario could not be certain. He was only sure that she had not been his server. She had not been the girl who had given him coffee to go.

To keep to a clean record, Judge Stittin asked if the defense wanted a continuance for a day or two to set forth their reasons on the record and what they wished to develop. Based on the waitress' statement, it would be difficult to document a reason to do so. At best, they could seek to interview her, but she had no obligation to respond to their inquiries. Obviously, the state had so advised her, intimating as they did so for her not to cooperate should this come to pass. They could check her background, but unless she was a convicted felon, it would not be relevant to her credibility, so any such details that were only of interest would be excluded. They could also risk asking her such questions now, but the likelihood of it boomeranging if she was not dirty was overwhelming. Clearly, if she had been bought—put up to telling a fairy tale—she wasn't going to confess it … in for a penny, in for a pound. Hawkins made a trial decision to move forward, as defense lawyers do. If he took the adjournment bait and it was granted but he came back to trial empty-handed, it would only reinforce her credibility.

Vickie Trucker's testimony was brief and telling. She was a former exotic bar dancer and looked like she belonged at Hooters and not some roadside diner. She was an unwed mother who had befriended her baby's father as a lap dancing customer. Happily for her, he was a man of very substantial means who owned a chain of six national fast food franchises in Mississippi and came from a wealthy family with a trust fund to boot. He had actually been fun for a while, but he was too straight arrow for her. When the baby came along, he did not step up to the plate for marriage. They went their separate ways. At the birthing at the hospital, the delivery team nurse, experienced in such unwed mother problems, dragged out his admission of fatherhood and duly completed the birth certificate, noting him to be the father. So arose an obligation of support.

Vickie extracted child support of one thousand dollars per week, which was much less profit than he received from any one of his fast food enterprises. Because she had no taxes to pay for child support, she was on easy street for the rest of her life and had no need to work. She could be a stay-at-home mom and cater to her own needs and fantasies, leaving aside forever those of her baby's daddy, who was ancient history except for her weekly check. Such was her background.

She had filled in at the diner before for a former dancing mate now turned waitress because the other woman's husband had insisted on a career change. It had happened only a few times before the night in question. She had done it because she found it somewhat amusing, especially since it was only an occasional cameo appearance and more so because she owed it to her friend. The how and the why of the debt was never explained. It was far afield and not relevant.

She showed up at the diner just before five p.m. for the dinner crowd. Within the hour, she saw Rosario come in. They were hardly busy, and she thought him attractive, so she watched him. He sat at the table of another waitress she didn't know and ordered. Then he went to the bathroom, presumably to wash up, leaving his backpack at the table. The diner was small enough that it required only one washroom. She went to use it too, hoping to bump into him, perhaps learn more about him while chatting him up to get know him if he kept her interest. *All work and no play makes…* she had thought. There were worse places to meet someone. She didn't want him to see her as the gravy train, because she had a good income but rather a good-looking waitress who had been standing on her little feet all day, looking to meet a nice guy.

She couldn't even bump into him. When she made her move, he deftly sidestepped her like a matador passing a bull. He was more wide awake and agile than she had thought. She misperceived that she would be the quick one and put the move or the jump on him. As they were doing their dance, though, she felt something about him was wrong. But she couldn't put her finger on it.

She went on to wash up. When she did, she saw the wastebasket was open. It was full. The top brown paper towels were wet and stained with smears of red. *Blood,* she had thought. The basin had touches of it too and was wet. Blood smears were up where the handles were; they were not as clear as the stains on the towels, but she thought there was no mistaking it. She was happy that she had missed meeting him. There was no taking up with him. He was either dirty or mean, even if handsome, and he kept some dark secret, she thought to herself then.

When she came out, she still had no customers to wait on. The place was much slower than it had been the few times before, and there was nothing to do, which was fine with her. The game of being a poor church mouse diner waitress no longer held any fascination for her. Sure, it was honest, clean work and more decent than taking off your clothes and dragging men (and these women) into the honey trap. But it was dull and boring, without any sense of adventure. Do two days waitressing in a row, and she would already be stuck in a hopeless rut.

She had time on her hands to unravel what else was wrong with this man's picture. That had been her strong point, even back in her early school days. Her mind could always spot what was out of order—too many fingers, a bald kid, no earlobes. So she studied the stranger up and down carefully, not like before when she had only focused on his blue-eyed, blond-haired, trim, wiry, good-looking features. Then she got it: his shirt. She had never seen it before, and she was surprised it hadn't hit her at once. Maybe she was losing her skills of observation or allowing herself to be taken in by just another pretty face. She had thought she was no longer sharp as a tack, getting senile too early. It was time to sharpen her power of observation and learn again to take it all in and not just focus on the bits and pieces that interested her.

His shirt was inside out. It had been buttoned with the buttons facing the inside, touching his skin. Looking carefully, she noticed the sewn seam where the fabric for the arms had been sewn to the shirt shoulder. She thought he was concealing something on the front of the shirt. Otherwise, he was some cool, fashion dude prancing in some new West Coast avant-garde dress style that hadn't hit the South yet. No, he was hiding something. Then she thought it was probably more blood.

She had lost interest just as an old couple had come in and taken one of her tables. She hadn't thought about him again until the detectives had contacted her the day before and visited her at once. Or so she said. End of story. Her testimony was a wrap.

Point, set, match to her, Rosario thought. But it was *merde*, pure bullshit. Now he knew for sure that he had never seen her before. There had been no cutie waitresses at that place, just big beef. After all, his mission going south had been looking for a wife. He would not have missed her.

Lastly, no one had danced with him at any bathroom door. That was for sure. It never happened. Legionnaires don't need hot and cold running water. They were nature boys trained to live in the woods and eat leaves and the berries they knew. They were also studied in grasses and roots and taught to find water in a desert—outdoorsmen. Did a bear shit in the woods? How about a legionnaire? Goddamn right they did! He had never washed up and sashayed by her. No one would have gotten close enough. It violated his training. Women were as dangerous as men, as he had learned in the hard bars of the world. They could stick people more quickly and easily than any man, taking them in charmingly. If a woman took down a legionnaire in the ranks, he would never outlive it. He would be called "girlie" forever. No, it had never happened. Before it could be all over, he was going to chat with her about the tooth fairy and her bullshit testimony, which he was sure would sink him. How right he was.

Hawkins couldn't touch her on cross-examination. She was practiced and a great witness. She took her time, looking like she was thinking and trying to be sure to tell the truth. She was right out of central casting. The more Hawkins tried, the deeper her calm answers put the hook in. He gave it up as quickly as he could, not even trying to score on her, knowing it was useless and harmful.

Rosario was not called. He had nothing to say that was positive, only denials. It would be his word against theirs if need be or just the plain old, "I didn't do it." Yes, he had been there. Yes, he was a killer by trade. No, he didn't recall dancing with Miss Lap-Dancer-Maneater. It would be useless and, worst of all, deadly. He was not going to be believed by these hometown jury boys. There was no way out now, no way to help himself. This last-minute surprise witness had ended any chance of nonconviction. Even if they had wanted six months to start the trial dance, it would have been the same eleventh-hour deal. The testimony was over. Summations were brief. There was not a whole lot to say.

There was no recess. Judge Stittin was well practiced. He had done it often enough. He didn't need any time to figure out his jury charges or reconcile those of both lawyers. He let the jury off for lunch and charged them at one thirty in the afternoon for forty-five minutes. From the fourteen jurors, the bailiff picked the foreman and eleven others to sit with the two standby alternates from the numbers cage. The jury retired at 2:35 p.m. It returned with a verdict before three p.m.: "Guilty of murder as charged." The judge polled the jurors. All agreed.

Some states investigate the convicted, not Mississippi, not in Judge Stittin's court. There was no presentence report. The defendant got convicted. He got sentenced. There was no lingering around.

It was getting late in the day. Everyone was worn out. The pumping of adrenalin was over. Sentencing was the final swan song. The fat lady had sung. Now it was Judge Stittin's turn, and he was not going to be long about it. He discharged the jury, but atypically, he had not thanked them for their service. His demeanor was bristling, angry.

He started right up, "Let me tell you, Mr. State's Attorney, that this is the flimsiest case I have ever seen in thirty-two years of criminal practice. From the outset, it appears clear to me that your office brought the case without any reliable proof linking the defendant to the offenses charged. This continued until the third day of a four-day, triple murder trial, when the state came up with Ms. Trucker to save the day like Mighty Mouse. Without her, you could not have survived a dismissal motion. Only she was the most circumstantial of evidence who seemingly linked the defendant to the offenses with her perceptions. Absent corroboration, it still remains most circumstantial.

"I thought about overruling the jury verdict, *sua sponte,* on the court's own motion. I won't do that, because I believe most of all in the jury system, although I know well it is not infallible. However, the case law supports that circumstantial evidence alone can support a jury verdict even beyond a reasonable doubt, as required in a criminal, let alone a capital, case. The jury was so charged properly. They returned their verdict, but I am not pleased with their brief deliberation, as it affects this defendant's future. I am also mindful that he does not have to prove himself not guilty, although there was little he could have said on his own behalf to turn the tide in his favor under the circumstances of this case.

"Obviously, the crimes are horrific—young and older lives taken needlessly and seemingly without motive. However, the punishment must fit the crime. It's up to me alone, in my discretion and based on my feeling of the facts and the demeanor of this trial and the proofs at hand, to set the sentence. I have already said I will not discharge our jury's verdict. If I did, there could be no double jeopardy, no retrial. However, I remain very circumspect and seriously concerned about the tenuous merit of the prosecution and the heretofore elusive Ms. Trucker, who seemed, however, believable. Quite an accomplished witness. However, doubts or suspicious aside, I have no contrary evidence impairing her credibility, however questionable her testimony may be. I am compelled to accept it by applicable law.

"Bailiff, have the defendant stand while I sentence him. Sir, do you wish to address the court before I impose sentence? You have every right to do so. I have already expressed myself. I believe the state has failed to prove motive for the crimes as to a stranger landed the day of their occurrence. The jury could have believed you are a deviant joy killer, and only that would support the verdict. It does rise up from the nature of the crimes and the cross mutilations.

"Speak now or not. It's up to you."

"No, thank you, sir."

"I exercise my discretion in sentencing you. You have been convicted of three first-degree crimes of unpremeditated murder. The statutory guidelines permit a sentence of twenty to thirty years for each offense. While there are no free crimes, I am at liberty to run your convictions concurrently or back to back. This means you could serve up to ninety years. It is unlikely that you would survive such a sentence, given your age. Thirty years would see you into old age and no longer any likely harm to society, in my opinion, given such a long sentence.

"However, I have observed your demeanor during the trial. I see no anger in you, no malice. Also no remorse, but there would be none if you were truly innocent. Under the law and on the exercise of my discretion as a superior court judge of the honorable State of Mississippi, I can sentence you downward outside of the guidelines. Under a third-degree crime you are exposed to a sentence of ten to twenty years. However, I am not bound yet. My discretion allows me to deviate downward two tiers. Conversely, I could take you up one tier, but nothing exists above first degree except the death penalty, which only a jury can impose upon separate hearing if the State seeks it at the outset, which it elected not to do.

"I am sentencing you to an offense of the third degree with a range of five to ten years. Our law states the presumptive range to be seven and a half years, being the midway point. However, I have told you I will not and refuse to sentence you back to back, and your three convictions will be served concurrently and not run wild.

"Further, I have weighed, as I must, the aggravating factors and the mitigating factors. The aggravating factors I find include that these crimes of which you stand convicted are of the most violent nature involving loss of life, are particularly violent given the carvings and hangings postmortem, and as convicted, I must regard you as a danger to society and recognize your need to be incarcerated.

"However, I find that the mitigating factors are stronger overall, and so they outweigh the aggravating factors and allow me to lessen your sentence from the seven-and-a-half–year presumptive midrange sentence. I find that the state's case lacks proof of motive. I find that the case as begun, until well into the trial, would not have supported a conviction and that the defense was overwhelmed and surprised by the testimony of Ms. Trucker, even if it was admissible according to the state's explanation of her unveiling as a witness. I am obligated to accept it, in the absence of any evidence to the contrary, there being none.

"Finally, I rely on my findings of your demeanor, which I am able to include in your favor. I have the feel of the case, and I am able to include my determinations in the weighted factors, both mitigating and aggravating. Conversely, the law allows me to find your lack of remorse as an additional aggravating factor, but I have already stated that I find none adversely, as you have consistently maintained your innocence."

"Accordingly, I sentence you to the minimum possible term in state prison of a flat five years, all sentences to run concurrently. You shall be eligible for good time credits and fifty-six days in jail for time served. Under Mississippi law, you shall be eligible for release with good time upon serving one-third of your sentence. That means that you are to serve five hundred seventy-five days before your credit. After this partial term has been served, if you behave yourself, I can and do direct the parole board of the Bureau of Prisons to release you without further hearing or proceedings. If they do not do so, you should contact your attorney, Mr. Hawthorne, and direct him to petition me, and I will rule on your release. You may appeal this sentence and your conviction. I am directing your public defender to advise you how to do so, although he should advise you whether to do it or not. You should think carefully whether to accept his counsel. If you want new counsel to help you decide, you may petition this court. Do you understand me?"

"Yes, sir."

"Do you understand me, Mr. Hawthorne, as his public defender?"

"Yes, judge."

"Court is dismissed, and the defendant is remanded to the custody of the superintendent of the Mississippi Bureau of Prisons. Court dismissed. Clear the courtroom, bailiff. Hold the defendant and counsel present. Off the record, madam recorder. Are we off the record now?"

"Yes, judge." was her prompt reply. She knew her judge and what was coming after five years in his court, eating his cake and drinking coffee in his chambers. She knew him to be a good and fair man. It was his turn now. A dressing down was at hand.

"Normally, I would do this at sidebar, but I have elected not to do so. It's enough we have gone off the record. The three of us are lawyers, Mr. Public Defender and Mr. Prosecutor. Let me tell you, Mr. Staggers, Esq., in front of those present, that I have known Mr. Curtis, Esq., the state's attorney of Mississippi, for years. Before our public service, we have both been counsel in the same office and adversaries. I tell you, and you may tell him as I will when next we meet, that you would do well never to appear before me again. You have obtained your conviction, but the *how* and the *why* of it disturbs me greatly. I remain, however, empty-handed. I have no facts, proofs, or evidence to take to your chief or the ethics committee or your supervisors other than a bad taste in my mouth and a pervasive feeling of judicial discomfort as to what has occurred in my courtroom. I decline to say more at this time.

"However, I believe further comment—let's say words of caution—are due you. I have observed this defendant. I have remarked on his sense of presence, his demeanor. I doubt you have. Perhaps you lack the ability to evaluate your fellow man.

"Does this man fit the bill of a serial killer? Hardly. For a foreigner, he speaks a mighty good American English. He is clearly smart and obviously well educated. He enjoys a distinct sophistication, and I suspect that his intellect and skills may well be more sophisticated than ours. He is no John Everyman walking in the park. This man can, and I believe will, prove to be a thorn in one's side come tomorrow. Not my side but yours, Mr. Prosecutor. I advise you if you have been out of bounds to consider moving the court to purge yourself and seek the forgiveness of this man. Let me say that 'if the shoe fits, wear it.' It's better to stumble than to fall. Enough said. A word to the wise should be sufficient. If you have not been smartened up now, you never will be, sir.

"Clear the court, Mr. Bailiff. Remove the defendant."

CHAPTER SEVEN
State Prison

Jails are for waiting trial and small crime convictions. Rosario was on his way instead to state prison—down Biloxi Way. It was out in the swampland, not so far from the bayous that Rosario had started out for. Still, it was a short fall by a long shot, even if he was doing only a year and a half.

On his arrival, Rosario changed from his jail orange clothes to blues clearly marked "Prison" with a big black bull's-eye target on the shirt back. There were no long sleeves, so the guards could see your hands, making it far more difficult to conceal a shiv or other weapon.

Protocol on arrival was for all incoming inmates to see the warden. There was little turnover. The prison held fewer than five hundred men, all of whom had been convicted of crimes of violence or murder.

The swamp location was designed to keep the men inside by their own will—rather than risk the snakes, quicksand, or other critters in a futile effort to flee that invariably proved to be some form of suicide. No one tried anymore, and no one had made it out before, not ever. There was no need for walls, high steel, or barbed wire. The guards did not track escapees into the swamp. They let prisoners know that, someday, a gator hunter would bring in the remains to get the hundred-dollar verification of death reward. They said to try it; it was just one less mouth to feed as far as the State of Mississippi was concerned.

So Rosario was told by Warden Cain Kikes. Kikes was a large man, standing six feet two inches with a deeply tanned, ruddy complexion. There was nothing friendly or redeeming about his visage or appearance. He was declared by both guards and inmates to be a mean, Baptist, anti-Catholic, nigger- and Jew-hating man who feared no one.

Rosario had no fear of him. He knew that he could walk out any day he wanted—alone or with some of his legion comrades he could summon up to speed him along. He also felt Warden Kikes' breathing was scared when they first met on intake day. Rosario thought he looked like a scared dog. He knew in his core that Kikes was put off by him.

"Well, boy, what are we going to do with your sorry ass, even if it's only for a year and a half? Shortest-term prisoner I ever got by far. Judge was clear about when you get out, so there's not much for me to do while seeing to your rehabilitation. We deal punishment here; break the rules and you'll find out, even if I can't up your time unless you commit another crime here. I can punish you though, boy, and given the chance, I'll break you. Done it plenty before to other stone-cold killers. Don't think much of killers, boy, especially the crazy child killers. That's you, boy.

"Most of the other men here think likewise, both guards and inmates. You have to watch your own back. Make your own way. No help from me, boy, so don't come crying if you slip in the shower. You got yourself in here, and you can see to your own way of surviving until you get out, if you make it that long.

"So what do you think we should do with you? Nothing easy going on here, not for violent killers. Plenty of hard work to do if you're good with an ax or a shovel. What are you good with other than a carving knife? No need for crosses here. Not many Christians here, boy. We don't go for the 'just discovered God' routine. No Muslim or Jew food on the menu. Don't bother going holy on me. 'cause there's nothing to gain. Get your reward in paradise. Not at my Biloxi prison. The 'con' don't work here, son. Not with me and not with the other men. You'll only harm yourself trying it. So speak up now. What are you good for?"

"The infirmary," Rosario came back in a firm, level, low-toned voice—

no hesitation, just waiting for the man to talk himself dry finally and shut up with all his warnings of fear.

"The infirmary, boy? What are you some kind of medicine man or just looking for a cushy job out of the rain?"

"Not here."

"What's that mean?"

"I'm not a doctor here."

"You letting me know that you are some sort of doctor? I read your file; no one knows who or what you are. Just a real mystery man. Now you're a doctor. A child-murdering doctor? That's a new one for me, even after thirty years on this job. Met all sorts but never a child-killing medicine man."

"I'm no killer. You know it, and Judge Stittin knew it. The fact is, I got convicted by a Mississippi closed-thinking jury, and that is what put me here."

"There's that, boy. Some of what you say rings true. We have plenty of time to sort it out. Let me tell you we have a doctor already, Doc Ruly. He comes twice a week Tuesday and Friday afternoons, sober or drunk. I've never seen him sober. Been told it happens but never when I see him. Drinks when he is here. He is all we got, and the men need to be more than half dead before they line up for him. Prison work is all he's got. Not fit for a hospital. His wife's brother is a big shot up in Jackson. Got him a state job years ago. He has tenure now, so we can't cut him loose. Only man on the job. He's got no notion to retire. He's got nothing else to do but drink, and the job don't stop him from that.

"I'd put you on the job and wait a few weeks to see what the doc says about you. Problem is, I wouldn't believe a thing he says. Here is what I am going to do. I'm going to put you there and see what the men say, see if they start lining up, getting their nerve back to get treated. It could prove to be a savior. Problem been, till now, that avoiding Doc Ruly means they just get worse, sicker. Then we send them out to be hospitalized and treated. It runs up the budget terrible, and it don't look good on my reports to the Bureau of Prisons. I got no choice though. Those federal judges say we got to treat them good with medicine and hospitals or we are violating their rights and we gonna get sued. No cure there. Okay with you, boy? Run a trial, put you on probation for a few weeks, see how you do?"

"Sure. Good by me, warden."

"Now I got to tell you, Jud Brotherman is the infirmary orderly. Been there twelve years. He's also the barber. Cuts hair or trims you, bathes and patches you up. He won't like you jumping over him, having just arrived and all. He's doing twenty-five on account of murder. Cut down his own parents and a sister. He's just about halfway through his sentence. No good time. Otherwise, he's a decent man, knows his limits. I bet, if you can deliver, he will work with you, knowing it's good for the men. I'll talk him up. You lodge there. I'll tell Assistant Warden Taylor to bring you in and send Brotherman to me now. Good luck, and I mean that for all of us. Don't let me down. Don't let the men down. If you find you can't handle it, speak right up, and we will get it fixed as best we can. Deal, boy?"

"Deal, warden."

The Warden left the room, hoping to Christ that the boy could cut the mustard, ending Doc Ruly's plague and helping the budget while healing the men. Rosario left knowing he would. Their deal was sealed.

Assistant Warden Taylor was a frail, sharp-nosed, pale weasel of a man with a soprano voice. He was a simply emotionless man of few words. He peeked in at the interview room door, otherwise not presenting himself or his authority. He squeaked out, "Follow me." Normally, he would bunk a new prisoner in one of the bunk beds in a common room holding two-tier bunk beds for twenty men and a side bathroom with two sinks and two toilets in open stalls. There were no showers and no cooking facilities. Taylor would send the prisoner for linens, a blanket, and a pillow. Each man had a metal factory-type locker and nothing more.

The infirmary was a much better deal. It took eight minutes to walk there, because it was on the other side of the camp from the warden's building which was next to the warden's private, fenced-in residence. The warden's house was secured by a double-gated entranceway that was opened and closed by an armed officer in an air-conditioned guard shack. State-of-the-art security cameras protected the entire perimeter, the residence approaches, and its interior. A six-car garage had security quarters on a second floor that were occupied around the clock by two more well-armed security officers who also monitored the cameras.

The infirmary sat by itself on a small rise. After three steps up, they reached a large wraparound porch with sunning chairs for the sick or for those waiting to be treated. There were exits at the ends of the side porches. The building ran nearly a hundred feet long and fifty feet wide on single story. Inside was a three-walled, benched waiting area separated by a courtroom–like railing with swinging double doors used by the men when called from the sign-in list. There was hot coffee and tea service for those waiting. Just inside the rail was a large plank table with six chairs and hand sinks on both sides with counters and top and bottom cabinets that were covered with clear glass so he could see the supplies, medicines, and bandages. The table held blood pressure cuffs, tongue sticks, Band-Aid dispensers, cotton, alcohol, and a dispenser for needles of different gauges and sizes. A needle and soiled bandage hazmat disposal unit was on the wall next to a soap and towel dispenser to the right of each sink. The water was operated by foot pedals. Brotherman ran a clean and well-stocked ship.

In the rear of the room were two treatment rooms. There were doors to hallways on either side. On the right, the hall led to six double rooms for patients as well as one shower and two toilets. The left hall went to two bedrooms for staff, a small but full kitchen, a large laundry room, and a well-equipped surgery with operating ceiling lights and an array of surgical tools. A free-standing oxygen supply cylinder and defibrillator complemented the facility's completeness for most emergencies. There were saline and antibiotic drips but no blood or plasma supply. Out the back door was a small helipad for emergency transport but no helicopter. If needed for medical rescue, air transport could only be ordered in from the state police by the warden.

"Step aside, Brotherman. You've been replaced," weasel Taylor cried out with glee, knowing he shocked the twelve-year veteran. "Back to haircuts only for you. This man has passed you over. Warden's orders. Too bad for you! Meet the new boss. You'll like him. He's a killer too. Good company. I'm sure you two will get along fine. Show him the ropes, barber, but first get up to the warden's now, pronto! I'm off. No time for the likes of you two."

In a flash, he showed his back and popped outside, disappearing down the hall.

"Rosario," he said, putting his friendly right hand out.

"Brotherman. No first names for me," Brotherman said, standing pat and not reaching out. No hand shaking took place. Prisoners don't touch each other. They were not up to being friendly. No social etiquette was at hand.

"Why you, Rosario?"

"I'm a doctor. Fell on some bad luck that landed me here. I might as well help the men. Help each other. Good for you?"

"If it's straight, it's okay with me. Time will tell."

No more chitchat was at hand. Brotherman showed him to the empty bedroom. He also showed him the infirmary's layout and how it worked.

After a few days, they fell into a routine and Rosario made some changes. Clinic hours would run all day for seven days a week. Sickness and pain knew no schedule. If he could make it in or was carried to the front door, anyone sick or injured could ring the bell day or night, if they were closed. The operating room, which had not seen duty for years, was scrubbed and cleaned.

Within only a few days, word had spread. The sick started coming, and the warden was pleased that there was a real doctor, even if he was a prisoner. Medicines and a full array of pills, antibiotics, and other needed supplies were ordered in from the Bureau of Prisons from lists the warden received weekly from Rosario. Small surgeries were performed to set and cast broken bones, repair wounds, and all types of injuries that required cutting and bandaging. Brotherman learned to assist and change bandages, check urine, and even draw blood, which went out to the lab each night. A fax machine was installed for receiving laboratory results. The men stopped going out to the hospital and getting sicker because they were not being properly treated. The only slow periods were Tuesday and Friday afternoons. No one, even if sick as a dog, lined up to see Doc Ruly. He was out of business at Biloxi State Prison, even if he was not out of his job altogether.

Warden Kikes followed up with Rosario a few weeks later, as they had agreed. Probation was over. There was no need to hash anything out. The men he knew from the guards were talking Rosario up. Morale was up, hospitalizations were down, and the population's health was improving. Prisoners were not shipping out to the hospital for broken bones, and Rosario somehow knew how to triage them without x-ray. The warden wondered how and where Rosario had learned that, never thinking at a Legionnaire MASH field unit. When the request came a month later for a small x-ray unit and a cardiograph machine, Warden Kikes made sure these requests were filled on an "as soon as possible" basis by the Bureau of Prisons. He even put in a request to the director of the Bureau of Prisons to send him a convict dentist (if they had one), seeing it as the way of the future.

Within the first month, the guards and their wives and children started coming to the clinic to get their bangs and bruises fixed up or to be diagnosed and medicated. It was quicker, easier, and cheaper. If Rosario couldn't help them, he was outspoken, telling them how soon they needed to see the specialist or get a follow-up and with what type of specialist. The warden told him to use the fax's phone and gave him a phone book and the Biloxi Hospital medical directory. He asked Rosario to refer all of the patients—guards and convicts alike—to physicians Rosario selected and to prime them on his opinions of what they needed for evaluation or treatment. Rosario did, and he developed a referring physician pool, and he received their treatment and laboratory reports, opening his own charts on each patient.

Two months in, the warden whose own family was seeing Rosario for various ailments, asked Rosario to dinner. Rosario thought it over rather than currying favor by agreeing at once. He declined politely. Trusting that Rosario had a good, well-deliberated reason, the warden asked him why. Rosario answered that word of it would spread in the population, and it would undercut his own image with the men. Treating staff was one thing. They were all isolated in the outback. Tough conditions were suffered by all. It made sense. Eating at the Warden's house was another thing. It was still the game of cops and robbers. The men would see it as a transgression. The warden understood. He had never thought to look at things from the convict's point of view. It was a rebirth of thought. He learned to look at both sides when making a key decision in the future. It became part of his learning curve. He saw it as Rosario's gift to him. Everyone, except perhaps Assistant Warden Taylor, seemed to come out better for knowing Rosario, growing from his advice and ministrations. The warden opined that, if Rosario could not come to the mountaintop, then it would come to him.

Sunday was a day of rest in all Mississippi prisons. Church services ended at noon. Dinner was served early for the men. So the infirmary was shut down after lunch hours on late Sunday afternoons.

The warden and his family went to the clinic, bringing food, drink, and silverware, and took their evening meal with Rosario and Brotherman at the treatment table without guards. The conversation was free and included all topics—politics, economy, morals, gossip, books, literature, and travel. Prison topics did not arise. Personal stories of growth and learning emerged. The warden's two children, Joshua (age fourteen) and Sara (a full year and a half younger), spoke up freely too. Everyone's speaking or opinion was respected. There was no overspeaking or disagreement. All opinions or utterances were equal. It was what they each valued that was important.

Sara spoke first. The warden and his wife and son had thought about it, but they were too polite.

"Where are you from, Rosario? How did you learn to doctor?" Her innocence was speaking; she was not yet old enough to understand that it might not be a proper question. She sounded like the young child with a crush on Clint Eastwood in *Pale Rider,* almost in love with the preacher/drifter/hero as he was leaving his good deeds done. Her inquiring voice was nearly the same.

For the first time since hitting the ground (hiking if not running) in Mississippi, Rosario was brought up tight, not replying right off. These people had become friends and no longer just more people he knew. Still they owed each other nothing, except perhaps words truly spoken or even not to be spoken. Sara had planted a fork in the road. Deciding which way to go required some hesitation and thought. Stop or go? There was no challenge in the question. It was a pure child's question. It meant no harm.

"It stays here," he said to Brotherman, not waiting for a reply and so showing him respect and trust. Everyone nodded, knowing they were about to share his secrets.

"Sara, I was born in Paris, and my family traveled all over the world when I was young. My father worked for the French government. At your age, I went to boarding school in Switzerland, and when I was Josh's age, my parents died; they were murdered." He lay it all out for them—medical school, the legion, war, killing, traveling to Mississippi, not killing anyone, the trial—down to, "Here we are."

It took a good half hour with no one interrupting. They were all hanging onto every spoken detail. Then he went into the future, sharing with her that, someday, he would take to the road again, but before he did he would explore whose place in jail he had taken and why—payback time. He only left out that he could well afford to do so. Rich man, poor man, beggar, thief—it was not their business. They had no need to know that he could easily afford to do what he wanted, probably banking a clear two million while in prison.

The seasons passed, and soon enough, it was fall again, marking a year since Rosario had de-planed. Warden Kikes came to visit Rosario the next day at the clinic, alone for the first time. The climate in the prison had definitely changed for the better. It was for the common good of all the prisoners and jailers who marked time there. No deep undercurrent of nervous unrest still existed. He knew damn well that the catalyst had been Rosario and his implementation of real medical care. Although "Doc" (as the men called him) did not mainstream in the general population, serving his time exclusively at the infirmary, he was nevertheless the prime behavioral role model who adjusted the mind-sets of those in the general population. They had traded in their attitudes of complaining, malingering, and malcontent to become do-gooders, helping out the weaker or needy among their fellow men. The change was not exactly overnight, but over the long winter and summer months now past, the metamorphosis had developed among some of the most hardened men. For sure, not everyone had been so positively affected, but the majority had been. The result was that the unchanged prisoners were isolated further by their negative acts. They were no longer feared or revered. Their influence was all but gone.

Better days had come so far along that, Warden Kikes could walk alone, unconcerned, among the men. He knew full well that no other warden in Mississippi could do so, and he doubted it occurred in other more distant penal institutions in America. It was a small benchmark, but it pleased him greatly.

When he had nearly arrived at the infirmary, he saw Rosario sitting on the front porch, coffee cup in hand. He called his greeting on approach and got one back as quickly.

"Pull up a chair, warden. Sit a while. It's a peaceful day, and the sun is still strong."

"You look nearly retired, Rosario."

"Brotherman is hovering like a nursemaid over the few patients we have in the ward. He's intent on doing his full share, and he has really learned a lot. Except for the surgery, there is little he can't do or won't try. He can pretty much do it all without me after the next six months."

"Sooner than that, Rosario. That's what I came to tell you. I'm kicking you out early. No need for you to be here, except to help the men, and that would be at your own expense. It's time for you to get on with it … whatever you have in mind. Not my business."

"I still have time to serve, warden. Judge Stittin was clear about the length of the sentence and the good time."

"Right you are, Rosario, but I too have discretion under Mississippi law. I'm not sure it exists elsewhere, but it's on the books. I've never heard of it being done. Wardens would think themselves weak if they used it. Truth is, I can cut your time by days, weeks, or months as I see fit—up to one-third of your sentence. I need give no reasons, just sign the paperwork. It's already prepared, and the way I figure it, you're out in seven days, but I'm waiting eight so no college boy at the Bureau of Prison jumps up and shouts that my math is wrong. The law was developed to help in dire situations. Let's say to bargain for a guard's life during a riot or lockdown. As they wrote it, I do not need any emerging. Just my own say so.

"You've done a lot for me, for the men on both sides of this place, and for the climate of the whole institution. Most men who are misjudged and locked up when innocent are embittered and angered. Like your trial judge, I feel you are just convicted but otherwise innocent. That's why I'm putting you out and not taking up more of your time needlessly. No sense talking about it. My mind's made up, but you go in a week and a day. Get yourself ready to leave. You can tell whomever you want or not. That's up to you. I don't particularly appreciate Assistant Warden Taylor, so I'm not advising him yet. It's none of his business. I want no pains in the ass or disruption.

"You get out a week from Tuesday morning, after the court is out. I'm taking you out by transport from the infirmary by the back gate. I will escort you as far as Highway Fifty-Five, about twelve miles from here. The boys will take you into Biloxi and keep you at the Greyhound station. You can get your arrest clothes back if you want. Otherwise, we give you new work clothes and fifty dollars, along with your poke that traveled with you when you were arrested. We both know you got enough in there to take a limo to wherever you want to go. You'll get your passport back and your original return flight Delta ticket, but in a few days, it will be out of date. Anything else you need to know?"

"No, warden. Thank you."

"You're more than welcome, Rosario. I've never said it before. If you get bored, come visit. If you want, I'll get the state's attorney general to look into getting you a real MD license on a waiver. It's been done before, I hear. I looked into it. It's a political thing, and I bet Judge Stittin will come on board, too, if I chat him up. Now I'm off. Thank you too, Rosario."

There was nothing more for either man to say.

CHAPTER EIGHT
Getting Out

Rosario never thought he would get out so soon. He had not been lax about it however. Rather, he had been his usual diligent self, always ahead of the curve, never really at peace. Instead, he was always controlling a nervous anxiousness that had been with him since boarding school, rising up in him from time to time after his parents' murders. It was a good and a bad thing. On the one hand, it was unsettling, disturbing his inner peace and never allowing him to be fully at rest. On the other hand, it kept him ever ready for all the curveballs of life. It made him stay alert and on his toes. There was no sneaking up on him, even with early release. He was still a good full step ahead of the shoeshine.

Well over a month before, he had contacted a few good men, seeing who was up for a job. These fellow legionnaires were older and hardened combat paratroopers. All of them were lifers on their second or third tours. Unlike a first-tour man, they could abort their tour, even for a year or two, still owing the balance on return while keeping their rank and all service credits. It let them help family or comrades as they alone saw fit. They had no need for permission; they just put in their papers. When they finished, they could return early or late just by appearing at their last deployment headquarters and taking any physical exams passed over during their absence.

Fitness was always a legionnaire's ticket to service. He could be bounced midtour if he could not meet medical fitness standards. It was the sole disqualifier and even the most errant behavior, including criminality (except against the legion), was no disqualifier. Indeed, crime was not even a talking point whether rape, murder, or arson. The legion did not turn its men over to become victims of civilian law. Rather, it promptly turned the other cheek by placing a man beyond reach, far, far away under a different name and history. If need be, the legion used its plastic surgeons to alter his appearance, including the fingerprints, by scalpel and acid. Those sought-after soldiers simply disappeared.

Rosario's option of mustering up his friends had been available both before and after prison. He had opted not to walk out. When freshly convicted and arrived in Biloxi, he had viewed it as more of a vacation and growth experience due to the diminished sentence. It had turned out overall to be due to the infirmary, and he had developed with good deeds. He had learned about the curse of the truly disenfranchised man and the nature of the prison beast. He found many of them as human beings to be superior to ordinary members of society who were at least as dishonest and a lot more untrustworthy. A convict's spoken pledge was usually sacrosanct and honored no matter what pitfalls developed in meeting it.

All of the men from the legion he had sought out were ready to go, and each responded accordingly. This left Rosario free to plan how to move forward. Each of his comrades-in-arms had different skills, which would be needed at different stages as his investigation moved forward. Each would have to be involved either out in the open or undercover, using various skills. The bottom line was that each man was well schooled in his developed talents and that each was known and trusted by the others, so they were also able to work together as a unit.

Knowing who was onboard allowed Rosario to strategize how to go about getting to the bottom of things for payback time. His mind was still calculating, as though he was planning out the various steps in a complicated field surgery on a man just brought in half alive who was dying in front of him with every minute that passed. For himself, his planning could be more leisurely; he could enjoy time for both reflection and refinement. The end result would be the same: find out who had fragged him and why and then extract full retribution and punishment, including, if proper, "termination with extreme prejudice" ... probably slowly. This full measure of harm depended upon who the person was and what role he played in the acts committed against him and the three original victims. Rosario well understood that there was a loose killer as well as those who assisted him either before or after his murders.

A conspiracy had developed to lay it at Rosario's doorstep simply due to his appearance and availability at the scene, which had been so opportune for them. It had simply been bad luck for him and fortunate for those really guilty. What had never struck them was that their game might per chance run afoul, because they had picked the wrong man—the right idea, but the wrong result—never thinking it could come back to haunt them. Bad news now: payback time was coming their way.

Rosario set his sails correctly, just like a TV movie, using the map pins of victims or events. In his active mind, he mulled over what he did and didn't know.

The easiest was that there were three people murdered and not by him. It had been done just as he was passing by, because he knew well that no victims had been hanging as he went by. Only he and the murder and accomplices all knew that Rosario didn't do it. This was a fulcrum he would use against them, including perhaps leading them to their exposure by revealing themselves.

He knew their star witness Miss Vickie Trucker, the well-prepared Ms. Bump and Tell, was put up to it. She was a describer of events that never occurred. She had to be the weakest link. He had drawn her in like a moth to a flame, so when close enough to the truth, she would burn and crash. The obvious course would be to backtrack from her, unless she gave up her truth in full early on, moving their cursor of harm down quickly to the punishment phase. Maybe she would save herself by showing true remorse to get out of their harm's way only slightly singed but not burned permanently. If not, there would be no good-time credit for her, and she would pay a price equal to the others. However, "extreme prejudice" would likely need to occur in any event, because the killer, at least, had earned it three times over. The public had already been dealt his conviction. Rosario had no faith in the honor of Mississippi justice; he believed that at least some of the police were shielding the killer. Justice so perverted would linger. Rosario was not disposed to hand over the killer, only to see him use influence to walk away from the full penalty his crimes required.

Remembering the cross carvings, Rosario didn't need a medical degree to know that he had a real sick puppy on his hands. The killing of two children told him that even before the killer touched them up with satanic markings in a godly place. Indeed in the end, the killer would likely say God had told him to do it, even believing it. Yes, he was sick all right, sick in the head and not curable. Rosario doubted that there was a psychiatrist young enough to cure him even if they started now. Why bother? The killer would do it again, so he had to be taken out—stopped cold by being made cold and dead like his victims. He needed to have the life carved out of him. If he wanted godly acts, then he could be guided by the good book: "An eye for an eye" meant "A life for a life."

It is a sin, thought Rosario, *that he will only give up one life for the three he took. Perhaps his friends will contribute their own lives to help balance the scales of real justice.* Time would tell.

Rosario would sort it out with a little help from his friends. He thought peacefully to himself that the Bible teaches "Justice is mine sayeth the Lord," *And Rosario's,* he thought. It was time to get started. Payback time had come early that fall.

CHAPTER NINE

Moving On

It was just another sun-filled, warm, late autumn day nearly turned eighty already. By 11:15 a.m., the two-man prison guard detail had cut him loose, as promised, just in front of the Greyhound bus station in Biloxi, Mississippi. The drop-off a block away was a courtesy to him, so he would not be seen leaving a prison transport. His new tan work clothes and shoes would reveal him right away as a released convict. If he walked the block into the station on his own, he would likely be taken as a late season postharvest workman who had used his parting pay for a new traveling wardrobe on his way back home. He was already undercover, hiding his true persona and game plans.

Rosario could have taken a limo, as the warden had said. His clothes were cheap, but his wallet had his fifty dollars from the Mississippi prison and the several thousand more with which he had been hiking and nearly five thousand more in Barclay's traveler checks he had bought in the Paris currency exchange before he had left. This was money he did not need to squirrel away for some rainy day to come. He had plenty to see him through just on what he had banked during his troubles.

Rosario did not want to arrive in Jackson in a blur of flashy limousine behavior, calling more attention to himself. He had to return, because that was where everything had all come down and so where the answers lay. Limo or cabbing it up did not fit the program. It would have been a false start.

He bought a one-way bus ticket from Biloxi to Jackson, paying $26.50 and pulled back from the ticket window to wait for the two thirty p.m. departure. The trip would take two hours or more depending on traffic. It was midweek, so it should be clear sailing. The arrival terminal was downtown, but Rosario knew already where he was heading. He would keep a low profile if he could but not hide. He knew the citizens of Jackson still thought he was socked away in prison. They had no notice of his early release. Certainly, Warden Kikes was not going to give him up with a press release, even though they had never discussed it.

During the trial, he had been transported in and out of the courthouse downtown, and the one-way traffic patterns had sped him past a high-rise Holiday Inn. That was his destination. He could have stayed slightly out of town, either at reasonable hotel chains or at a spa near the county club, but he thought the security would be better in a high-rise facility where everyone had to come in through the main lobby and be seen and captured on camera.

He did not want visitors until the boys were online. With common protection, they could come or go like rain water. Rosario being snatched would no longer be part of the problem but rather part of the solution; his quarry would reveal themselves for the others to take down. He would only relocate later when the bases were covered.

Now he needed some time to readjust his senses after prison, get on a regular food schedule, learn to behave in public again, and get used to walking out the door a free man. He had to shed the inmate mentality. He also needed to develop a base for operations and work out the details of a safe house, more finances, transportation, weapons, backup food and medical supplies, how the men would come and go. There was plenty of startup work to do.

His list of needed things was long enough, and he logged it in mentally while making the ride. Happily, the bus was empty. It could hold over forty-eight people, including standees, on a long trip. That day, there were only six passengers, two of whom were the parents of two young children with whom they sat in the rear of the bus. The two others sat midway back on the left. Rosario sat in the front in the row behind the driver but on the other side, with the electric doorway in front facing out on the windshield, just like the driver but being on a better position. He nestled in, shut his eyes, and sat comfortably thinking enjoying the simple pleasure of being mobile again.

CHAPTER TEN

Getting Ready

The ride up didn't take two hours. It was quicker, the bus arriving early because there was no traffic. Maybe it was because there were only six passengers; they were traveling light, moving quicker, Rosario thought.

He was tired, not being accustomed to motor travel and getting weary as the time and miles passed. He used to fall asleep in cars as a child, and that was back again with him as an adult, briefly, he hoped. *Maybe,* he thought, *with no real concerns I am loosening up from the time in jail, having never let my defenses down until now.* Maybe it was the absence of adrenaline kicking through him constantly as he had stayed on guard that was finally letting his body key down and rest. It wasn't a feeling he disliked, but rather one he distrusted. It was never good to let his guard down, but he knew that it was necessary. Only if he could relax could he build back up to vital status, the constant awareness on full alert. He had slept the last hour into Jackson.

It wasn't the lack of motion that woke Rosario. It was the driver becoming conductor signing out over his intercom.

"Downtown Jackson. Last stop."

There had been no other stops. It cost him a little more, although 90 percent of the Biloxi-to-Jackson trips were nonstop. So the ticket master had told him in case he wanted the local or to save money. Only the first and last trips of the day (at six a.m. and nine p.m.) were locals. Mostly day travelers started out at daybreak and came home late at night after visiting friends or family or doing their business on the way in the small towns serviced. The difference was that passengers could signal their own stops with a rope buzzer and flag the bus down on the highway on the return.

"Women and children." was the Greyhound driver's next and only other call out. By then, Rosario was wide awake. He couldn't understand why Titanic departure rules applied to bus travelers, but he thought maybe it was some form of Southern politeness to let women and children de-bus first. The bus had no restroom, so maybe it was a way of allowing them to use the station facilities more quickly, bottoming to the Southern view that women were the weaker sex who, like children, needed all the preferential treatment that they could muster.

Rosario waited his turn. He was the last man off with no luggage to carry. He got a "Good night, mister," from the driver, who was just behind him, keying the switch to close the automatic door. Rosario got his bearings and started for State Street, which, he was certain, was only a few blocks to the right up a small incline. On the third block, he hit it, but the evening traffic was heavy, with both cars and pedestrians making their way home after the workday's end. Most of the cars were being driven by men alone—no carpooling here. The pedestrians were nearly all women, who were likely carless or saving on weekly downtown parking, because in the South, even he knew women were underappreciated and underpaid compared to men. It was the same in France and, really, throughout all of the civilized and uncivilized world where he had been. All the world's women were underdogs, mostly not even begging a fair shake. Mississippi was hardly the exception, but it became worse for blacks and much worse for black women who got it from all sides, including mostly their own men and boys.

Maybe he was looking for a black man gone crazy and killing, he thought, for the first time. He doubted it. Any black man would have to have a great amount of influence as a black, and killing whites was not acceptable. *No way*, he thought, immediately dismissing the notion. His prey was definitely white, rich, and probably from an established good-old-boy, well-aged Mississippi family. He would be no Catholic or Jew but a Baptist, living easily in the culture of Southern white life. He would be a churchgoer himself for sure—him and his family—sitting in the very front, applauded by their camp followers, who likely depended substantially on their patronage and social support.

Time would tell when he warmed up their popcorn kettle of life, adding enough oil and heat to the mix until they popped themselves into view. Then the game would really get started on the retribution scoreboard. It would be payback time, hurting time, and likely killing time. Time alone would tell, bearing witness and revealing such ultimate truths.

Rosario didn't know if he should turn left or right on State Street. He could ask one of the fine-looking, trim, and well-dressed, high-heeled local beauties. He didn't want to. Except for the warden's family, he had not conversed with women in over a year. He didn't want to restart by asking directions. That was too minimal.

Moreover, he was back on the streets, and he had to make his own way. He needed the sharpening of his own skills. It was easy. He waited for the green light and crossed midway, stopping to look up both sides of the street for a fourteen-story building. It was several more blocks down on the right, its distinctive green sign easy to see. Four minutes later, he was passing through the motion-censor doors and being struck by the oncoming air conditioning as he traveled the lobby concourse to the check-in counters. No other arrivals were at hand, and just a few people were sitting in the lobby, waiting to be joined or reading papers. He noted that the lobby piano barroom was well lit and covered. Most of the seats and tables were already occupied even so early in the evening.

Rosario made it about ten feet from the reservation arrival counter when an undernourished check-in clerk with bad skin shouted to him.

"Do you have a reservation tonight, sir?"

Rosario was reluctant to speak. While still approaching, he put on his pleasant set-them-at-ease smile, shaking his head in the negative.

"Well, we are not full, sir. Let's see what we can do to accommodate you. How many people will be staying?"

"Just me, please, young man."

"All right, sir, let me check the computer. Smoking or nonsmoking? King size bed or twins?"

"Do you have a secure floor with concierge service?"

"Yes, sir. The penthouse on the fourteenth floor, but there is no night service during the week Monday through Thursday after seven p.m. We are open until midnight on the weekends, but the prices are another twenty dollars per night for your Friday, Saturday or Sunday night stay. The weekday cost is one hundred seventy-five dollars, but if you book three nights or more and stay into the week, it is a flat one hundred fifty dollars per night no matter how long you stay. Best to book the whole stay in advance in case we fill up, which we sometimes do on football weekends this time of year."

"Good idea, young man. Thank you. I'll book two weeks now, in advance—concierge floor, king size, smoking, please." Rosario didn't smoke, but he could not recall if any of the crew did. If they met at the hotel at all, it would be best to provide for smoking rather than set off a too-sensitive smoke alarm in case they did smoke.

"Your charge at the minimum rate is two thousand one hundred dollars, sir, before state hotel tax. Is that all right with you?" The clerk had looked obviously for his baggage.

"Will anyone be staying with you? The rate is for single occupancy."

"No. Maybe a visitor but no guests. The price is fine. Are Barclay's traveler checks for full payment in advance, all right?"

"Certainly, sir. Will you need a card pass for the garage? No charge for parking for guests."

"Not at this time."

Rosario pulled out his blue plastic Barclay's check wallet and separated four five hundred–dollar checks, adding a one hundred dollar bill to it from his wallet. He only had five hundred–dollar checks and didn't want to get into a cash-back situation that would lead to any request for his passport or foreign driver's license. There was no need for more disclosure yet of who he was. He didn't think his name was a household name yet in Jackson, but someone might pick up on it. *Not too many Rosarios in Jackson lately,* he thought.

The clerk didn't answer but scooped up the money, ringing the doorman's bell.

"Luther will show you up and give you your special elevator access key card for the concierge floor. You can only get out on this floor with it. If you lose it, let us know. It happens all the time. We will change your door lock and give you a new key. Do you need any help with luggage, sir?" he asked, believing he knew the answer but still curious. Maybe he thought someone had driven Rosario and had the luggage still in the car. He would let Luther get a look at them and catch him up later about the stranger who was no Southerner.

"No, thank you. Off we go, Luther, please. I might as well get as much concierge time in as I can," Rosario said, sounding like a real traveling man who was accustomed to living off all the free hotel perks he could.

Up they went. Luther tried out some chitchat about a long trip and weather in Jackson and any plane trip in. Luther saw the deep sun from the last year's sun on Rosario's face, but it led him nowhere. All Rosario gave him was, "Just tired, Luther. Glad to bunk down early tonight, get room service, shower while I'm waiting, and then some TV and beddy-bye." It all sounded so normal.

Luther let him out of the elevator first, introduced him to the concierge, Jill, who muttered a welcoming to him and whisked him off to room 1414. He opened the door, fixed the air conditioning, asked about ice and if Rosario needed anything more. Rosario declined and gave Luther a ten dollar bill, showing he was no cheapskate. It was top class for Jackson; Rosario already knew money talked here. Luther gave him a real thank-you and shut the door properly, not slamming it. Rosario thought Luther even bowed a little, but he wasn't sure. Maybe it was just poor posture from long hours and aching bones on the old man. If push came to shove, though, he thought Luther would be a reliable resource if money smoothed the way.

He was up at six a.m. No clock was needed. Old habits died hard. His body was trained, and there was no sense trying to change it by hanging around in bed and hoping for another sleep cycle that would never come. On with the same clothes after a wake up morning shower – a continuing luxury allowed him from infirmary duty. It was now a morning ritual center piece of his daily wake up ablutions.

Rosario had to pass the word along to the boys but not from the hotel. There was no need for a hotel log of overseas phone calls. Instead he found a Western Union store using the Yellow Pages. It was only a few blocks away.

In fact, he learned on day one that everything in downtown Jackson was only a few blocks away. It had to be the smallest state capital in the United States. None could be smaller. A French countryside town was bigger. It was good he thought. Smaller was better. There would be less to wade through to get to the bottom of things. So much the better. If he tried it in Boston or Washington DC, where he had been as a child, it might prove to be a big undertaking and maybe not possible.

He went back to the Yellow Pages, this time looking for banks. He found three that interested him based on size, since they revealed in their advertisements all of their many branches. He wanted a big one—big banks said money and prestige. Who he banked with would say who he was to those who might do business with him or check him out, asking "Who's your banker? Which bank?"

Rosario downed a morning roll and hot black coffee. He greeted the day hostess and asked her to have his room made up early as he was on the way out.

He found the three banks easily and knew the choice could only be the First National Bank of Mississippi. It was the largest by far and nearly modern for Jackson. It had eight stories rather than the two or three of the others, and it was in sight of the State Capitol building.

Rosario had been his busiest in the last days before his release. Six days ago, he had put through three telephone calls in a row from the infirmary fax phone after midnight. That was the first and last time he had used the phone personally. No one would notice. He doubted anyone would even look at his charges, which would cost no more than twenty dollars in all with late night rates, direct dials, and less than a minute length each. Few words were needed between legionnaires. No names were used, and none were needed. Their phone numbers he knew. No phone books were required. One call was to Marseilles, another was to Algiers, and the last was to Mombassa. All went to answering devices to be serviced later. All the calls were the same with just a few words: "Trouble. Help. Merci. Regrets only, SVP." None came. All three friends were a go.

At the Western Union office, he sent them each the same telex to their legion posts, using the last four numbers from their legionnaire identification tags as addresses. "Fine day. Missing you. Thank you. Hidt."

It was an easy message to translate. "Fine day" had four letters first word: "See you in four days." "Missing you" meant "don't approach. I will come to you when I see you." "Hidt" used as his name was the location, which had to be a hotel. His telex was routed from Western Union in Jackson, Mississippi, with its downtown location. "HI" was the well-known American hotel chain, Holiday Inn. "DT" was downtown. It was an easy message and would be an easy find. There was no real chance to miss him. The game had begun. The boys were coming in. A day later, he would check for replies of regrets only, if any. He would learn that there were none.

Obviously, the men knew each other over the years of soldiering in various campaigns. What each didn't know was whom else Rosario had called in. They knew they would look up and form their group. They would spot each other, likely coming in to roost, without acknowledging each other until Rosario set the stage for their behavior.

It was still too early for a gentleman to be at a bank to do business. Eleven a.m. would be the earliest. He bought a coffee in a luncheonette, still black prison style. He was not yet ready to switch back to light crème and sugar that doctors drank endlessly on duty and off, needing the caffeine but buffering the stomach from the harms of a constant coffee drip.

He went shopping, roaming the downtown. From the windows of the many men's stores, it seemed that downtown Jackson was the Mississippi male fashion capital. There were very few women's stores, he noticed. The fairer sex relied upon malls or QVC specials. He was looking for style, trying to see what was repeated in the various store windows. He was looking for names too—not Mississippi trade names or old boy names.

Clothes were a statement, and he wanted the right one. He wanted some fashion advice. He needed an old-fashion tailor/shopkeeper. Paris still had them on Avenue Foch, and he thought so might Jackson. He felt should have checked the Yellow Pages. There was no need; he found one soon enough. "GOLDSTIEN & SONS, HABERDASHERS SINCE 1884" the sign read, adding "FINE MEN'S TAILORED CLOTHES." It was only eight-thirty, and the store was already open, while other stores were still locked and dark. In he went.

"Good morning, sir. Fine Mississippi sun already up today." The bent-over old Jew in his mid-seventies spoke to him, not knowing who he was, giving him a good local hello.

"I'm Goldstien the son. My brother is long gone, and my boy's a doctor. I'm the last of the breed, I'm afraid. How about coffee or tea or something cold to drink? It's too early for a beer, unless you say so."

"No, thank you, Mr. Goldstien, and it is a fine day. I'm in from the country and still in my work clothes. I need to meet my banker today, do some business. It's not an expected visit. I need to be ready to sit down about eleven so I can still move some funds before day's end. How about you fix me up?"

"My pleasure, sir. We need off-the-rack to meet your deadline. I can tailor it right up if need be," said Goldstien, pulling out a tape measure and beginning to see how to fit Rosario, not bothering to ask him his size. The old man was going over him with his practiced eye as well as his tape measure, noting it all down in his mind, no paper needed. "I think we should do the shirt first to be top dressed for the clothes and tie. Best to make a good impression. I think a dark lightweight suit. Either blue or brown would be best. Your choice though."

"No, I will be guided by you. You want to talk money and business, I'm your man." When it comes to clothes, you're in charge. I never was good at putting it all together."

Twenty minutes later, Goldstien had Rosario fully outfitted with a pocketless white shirt with cuffs, black onyx cufflinks, a dark royal blue poplin suit size forty-four, and a paler blue tie with a crossover red-lined motif. The shoes were a problem, because the choice was between only brown or black lace-ups. The brown fit better, but the black looked better, so black it was. Clothes made the man. The brown just didn't work better, fit or not. It was of no moment to Rosario; he didn't plan on using them much. Rosario asked for the bill, settled it, thanked the old man, and left his giveaway prison clothes to be picked up later.

He went back to the Western Union office, this time arranging a long-distance phone call to Zurich, Switzerland, to his private banker, who had managed his money ever since his parents had died. The banker, Hans Gruber, was a relative of his boarding school's headmaster through marriage. They had met many times over the years and Herr Gruber always insisted on educating Rosario about how well his investments had done since their last go-round. From his earliest days as a youth until his thirties, Rosario had always begged off, not really wanting the lecture. Gruber had had no choice but to defer. After all, old or not, Rosario was the customer. The bank where Gruber was a top-level officer prided itself on its customer relations, following the well-established rule that "The customer is always right," even if the bankers knew the customer was wrong. After all, it was the customer's money.

With moderate Swiss taxes and tax-free investments, the growth over the years had been from about six million to about twenty million US dollars net after expenses, payouts to Rosario, and most adequate bank fees. No one but the client and the banker knew the details in full, and no one would, due to Swiss banking privacy rules.

No government as creditor was getting at Rosario's money; they could not even identify the money to claim or lay a levy on. Moreover the bank had no retail offices or broad-access computers to be hacked. It existed only on one floor (the top floor) of a Bahnhofstrasse three-story building with one small sign outside. It had about twenty employees, but it enjoyed a vast base of old-money customers. It would not have accepted Rosario if it had not been for his parents' tragedy and the strong request of Gruber's older brother-in-law, Rosario's boarding school headmaster. However, once someone was a customer, there were no other qualifications needed. They all got the same full attention and investment advice.

Rosario had declined to receive it, which made Herr Gruber work just a little bit harder to benefit Rosario, knowing he enjoyed Rosario's full trust. He wanted no mistakes, no losses in his account. Indeed, he was the only one outside the legion who knew of Rosario's true identity, medical training, and background. Although he took no personal credit for it, he was pleased by Rosario's self-guided development, even if he thought Rosario's choice to be a soldier fell short of what he could accomplish.

Rosario bought a credit phone card and placed his call to Gruber's direct line, knowing he would answer unless sick or traveling. If so, it would forward to an assistant. Gruber came on the line quickly, and they exchanged greetings and small pleasantries briefly. It was still really about business.

Rosario told Gruber he was in Mississippi, wanting to arrange a transfer of funds of about four hundred thousand US dollars. He thought he would have a local banker call Gruber probably before his usual quitting time of seven p.m. All was clear, and there was nothing else to arrange, so he rang off with some few dollars still left on the card. He took the card out and bent it until the cheap plastic broke. He broke the halves again and threw the four plastic quarters away separately as he moved toward the bank.

The modern-on-the-outside building was the complete opposite inside. It went back decades, looking like a courtroom from the 1940s with old wood paneling and desks of the same period with green printer's lamps. The teller's cages were barred rather than Plexiglas from the mid-desk level with a small opening at the bottom to pass documents and money back and forth. The tellers had a dress code, and all wore white shirts and black pants or skirts. A majordomo, large black man in formal clothes, greeted him at the courtroom-gated entrance to the bank offices. He could not pass directly to the teller area.

Rosario approached the man and advised that he wanted to open an account. He was directed to a Ms. Stanford. Rosario deferred, saying he was accustomed to doing business with men.

"Certainly, sir," came the man's reply. He subtly agreed with a slight grin, saying he would check to see if Mr. Sinclair was available, telling Rosario that Mr. Sinclair was a senior vice president of the bank and the chief officer at the Jackson location.

Rosario did not have long to wait. Less than a minute later, a tallish but heavyset man dressed in an all-black suit bound out of the rear, moving quickly toward Rosario with a pleasant welcoming smile on his face.

"Arnot Sinclair, sir. At your service. How may I help you today?"

"Thank you for seeing me on such short notice, Mr. Sinclair. I have decided to go into business in town, and I would like to open an account with wired funds from my main bank in Zurich. Let's say four hundred thousand US dollars to start."

"Certainly, sir. I am sure we can accommodate you. Please join me in my office, where we can talk more comfortably."

Sinclair turned without hesitation or waiting for a reply, knowing that he would be followed. He returned to his office at the same quick pace and popped around behind his desk, motioning for Rosario to be seated in one of the two plush chairs that faced him from beyond the desk front. Rosario sat to the right.

"Something to drink, Mr. ... ?" said Sinclair leaving an impasse. There had been no real introduction before.

"Rosario, Mr. Sinclair. I am a French national, but I believe there is a good investment opportunity in Jackson. I am not yet sure what I wish to pursue, but I think that I shall do so soon enough. Therefore, it is best to have funds on hand. I have banked in Switzerland for years and years, and I am quite accustomed to your profession. My personal banker in Zurich is Herr Hans Gruber, director. He is still at work yet today, and I have called around to him to say someone would be calling. Let me ask you, please, to do so and give him the wire instructions. He will remit four hundred thousand dollars more or less, depending on which investment he has elected to liquidate upon my earlier instructions. I will sign whatever forms you need to accomplish this. I will draw on the funds as needed and seek your advice as to local matters or professionals as I require. Is that acceptable to you, Mr. Sinclair?"

"Most certainly, and I appreciate your direct style, Rosario. I too am mostly about business and otherwise a man of few words. Here is my card with my phone numbers for your convenience. Please feel free to contact me directly as your needs arise. Certainly, I can and will direct you to competent people locally. Let me have your passport to copy, and we will prepare the necessary papers and contact Director Gruber to make the forwarding arrangements. Do you have a local address?

"Thank you so much. Here are Herr Gruber's phone and telex numbers. I am currently on the concierge floor at the Holiday Inn downtown. Here is my passport. When shall I return to sign, or would you rather have the papers delivered to me and I will complete them and have them returned?"

"That's fine. No need to come back. We shall have them at the hotel's front desk in, say, an hour. If any issues arise, I shall leave you a message. Thank you for selecting our bank. May I speak frankly?"

"Certainly, Mr. Sinclair. That is what I would encourage to develop our relationship. Never hesitate to tell me what you think I need to know. You know best how things are done here, not I."

"Is nothing of substance, Mr. Rosario. Rather it is only a matter of my curiosity. It's something we discuss internally. I wonder what brought you to our doorstep, there being so many banks in town. Obviously, you are a man of substance and assets. Did we receive a recommendation? Do we have a mutual acquaintance to thank?"

"No, Mr. Sinclair. I'm self-starting and do it myself. I looked at the banks with downtown locations in the phone book and then physically at the banks themselves from the outside. I was guided by appearances, and yours seemed most appropriate. It was as simple as that. Normally, I would have just set forth at first only my needs and interviewed the others. I've elected not to do so, because I already feel comfortable here with your good attention.

"I will await the papers. I expect the transfer will be without issue, for which I thank you in advance. Have a good day," Rosario's said as he stood up and offered his hand. When the shaking was done, he simply departed, not needing to be shown out.

Rosario went back to the hotel to his made-up room, quickly changing back to the far more comfortable prison clothes, which he had picked up on the way back. He popped out to the concierge desk and met Julie, who had come on with the shift at noon. He asked for black coffee, fruit, and cheese, although it was nearby and he could have helped himself. He wanted to give her something to do and loosen her up a little bit before trying some chitchat.

She served it all up deftly in a few short minutes with the skill of a trained sous chef, making sure the plate was attractively arranged and without side spills of dragged food. Unlike before when he had been paying no real attention, he noticed that she was as attractive as the plate she served. She was well-coiffed and manicured. She stood only a few inches shorter than he did, probably because she was wearing low-cut Keds sneakers. He thought she might have him bested in height in high heels. Her clothes were black, creased, beltless silk pants and a matching shirt, all revealing her to be trim and in apparent good shape. She looked just plain healthy. She was thin-lipped and narrow in the face. Her hair was black, like her clothes, and put up in a school girl's ponytail. Her face revealed both inner confidence and apparent intelligence. Her demeanor was straightforward and open for approach, and verbally, she appeared able to hold her own in light and heavier conversation as he learned quickly.

He thanked her politely and began to eat his small meal with appreciation. He finished quickly and began his chitchat.

He learned that Julie was a recent graduate from Mississippi State University and was from Michigan. She liked the South and its warmer days and polite society, which she thought less backbiting and intense than the North. Jobs were scarce everywhere, even for an honor student in psychology. She had worked part-time at the hotel in reservations, working her way up to the fourteenth-floor concierge staff, which paid the best except for management positions. The guests were good tippers and, on the evening shift, doled out free food and drink; on the late weekend shifts, she said she could easily pocket a hundred or more in tips. She had decided to go full-time and make Jackson her home, at least for a while, giving herself time to decide whether to go on for a graduate degree, an MS or even a PhD. Either would be an expensive pursuit, but for education, she knew her parents would help her out all they could. She just didn't want to get started and spend their money only to put it aside later, not being fully committed to seeing the degree through. All this Rosario learned through just a few direct questions. In return, she asked nothing about him. He thought it too one-sided and almost strange.

As she spoke and the more he thought about it, he concluded it was her style. She didn't pry into the guests' stories. It was up to them to reveal themselves or not. She was probably tired of their boring tales and was loathe to encourage stories to be thrust upon her, thinking it was better to tell her own tales if asked. It was simpler and without any new burdens. Besides, what was he to tell her? Nothing about the legion or medicine. He could try her out with his being a few days out of jail as a locally convicted mass murderer and listen to her start screaming, remembering who he was. It would earn him nothing and had no benefits. He kept their dialogue away from himself.

Realizing she knew the local environment well after hearing her story, Rosario asked her what she thought Jackson itself was missing. She gave no quick reply and rather set about removing his dishes to a nearby kitchen area, returning promptly and sitting across from him, there being no other guests to help or serve.

"A good bar/restaurant," she said. He listened.

"Why? I think there would be plenty of those already."

"Yes, there are, but the key word in the sentence was 'good.'" She was coming back a little feisty. He liked that. *Speak right up, she did. No shyness. I asked her, and she thought about it and told me what she thought.* Now that he liked her style, he found it more attractive than her appearance. He knew a lot of other men, and most probably Southern men, would not appreciate her style, finding it too direct and possible emasculating. That was their problem and not his. He was spoiled. Why should she not be?

"How so?" he came back.

"There are a lot of saloons. All made holdouts. Beer and a cheap shot. They're not fit really for mixed company, unless you were a woman who has lost her way in life."

He was not sure what she meant. Tarts? He didn't ask. After all, he had started young himself with such women. The legion was certainly not a respite from such women. Rather, they were the legionnaires' favorite flavor. Hello, goodbye, and that was it—no real attachments. There might be some shared meals or long nights drinking, but that was it. There was no permanency, no real attachment.

"Go on, please. What else need I know? I'm thinking about going into business here. I would like to know what you think would be a success, draw the people in, make them happy while they spend their money, bring them back when they are bored, use them to get to the truth or the bottom line." He was to ferret out the truth, he thought, but he did not share it with her.

"Well, Mr. Gruber," she said, showing she knew his name from the daily arrival roster. "There are plenty of chains, but there are just the same old, same old. There's nothing novel about a hooters or a TGIF. Close your eyes and think; they wear the same design, taste, and style as in every other city. Go there once, and you've seen them all. It's really quite boring.

"Biker bars and redneck or motorcycle bars don't favor a mixed crowd or outsiders. They're not friendly at all unless you're just looking for a fight or a hospital visit. Also, what they serve is not food. That leaves the need for just a nice down-home place with a casual and open environment folks—say twenty-five to fifty—are likely to appreciate and hang out at, coming back happily time and again.

"I don't think price is an issue, but higher priced—even top drawer— would be better to keep the riffraff out. There is plenty of real money here. People here think going out to eat is its own form of entertainment, and they are willing to bear the cost of it, if they get what they want. Although, it says little for the customers, I've seen it here. Many people like to brag about the high prices they paid for last night's dinner and drinking. Rich people like to go to places others can't afford. Get the prices high enough to keep them out, and they flock to you. They have to show up even if they really can't afford it to be something they really are not."

Rosario was more than surprised about how much thought she had poured out in reply to a simple question. It was all good advice and analysis. She was quick-minded. Before he had thought her smart; now he knew she was.

"Thank you," he said. "Quite interesting. See you later. Talk again if it's okay with you," he said, politely placing a twenty dollar bill on the table not handing it to her directly—impersonal was better.

She started to decline the money, saying, "Not necessary," but he smiled politely at her briefly and turned away. He headed down the hallway to his corner room, not sure who had hooked whom, thinking that she might well have bested him with her candor.

Maybe she was right. A good bar restaurant could become quite an effective crossroad information highway, bringing them in to him and saving the going out looking for them. It was an approach he had not thought about before. She had opened his mind.

Now there was little to do while awaiting his friends, maybe a little research. He called the bell desk and ordered up all the local newspapers Jackson had to offer to learn if the classifieds offered any Jackson eateries for sale.

Herr Kroper was first in, coming from Zurich. Because of his appearance, many of the men believed he was a second-generation, postwar Nazi; they knew he came from wealth from Paraguay. It was rumored that his father had served Hitler personally as an assassin of his believed enemies during the last mad months in the Berlin bunker. He was to have fled with diamond riches in hand, taking the protected Vatican route out like so many other SS officers, posing as a priest while moving through the underground railroad and ending up safely rich in Latin America. Nothing else really was known of Kroper's background.

He was a bull of a man although not tall, standing only five feet eight inches. He was of wide girth. With his oversize, powerful hands, he was well able and accustomed to choking a man to death or snapping his neck. The legion was not given to criticism of the tactics of its men. The focus was on winning and staying alive. Had human rights been in order even in wartime, Kroper would have been court-martialed and mustered out early on for murder. He did not take prisoners. He interrogated them and put them down like sick dogs but with greater dispatch and less kindness. He used his hands to send his victims to hell. His prisoners did not know what lay in store, but his comrades did. Even as their company commander, he was only feared rather than liked, and yet no one moved against him, because he was a good officer. His instincts kept the men alive, and he was not an armchair warrior. He was always out front, risking his life before those of his men. He was charmed, because no harm befell him, and those who served under him came to believe that his karma would help to save them.

The men in the legion were issued standard weapons—pistols, assault rifles, and all sorts of knives. However, there was no restriction on the men coming and using their own weapons, most of which were superiorly designed to more effectively harm and kill. Different environments demanded tailored weapons to work with jungle rot, desert heat, or brutal cold. Clothes too were important, and private sources were better than the regular issue. Given the size of the legion and its multienvironment deployment, someone had to buy these specialized supplies, which the men could order up for little or no cost. Kroper was the supply man, buying in South Africa at favored prices when he got the call. He had passed the job onto another member of his procurement team to ready himself to go Stateside.

He pulled Jackson, Mississippi, up on the Internet and developed his travel route from South Africa to Berlin and then through to Miami with a Delta flight to Jackson. He traveled on a German passport purchased years ago that listed his profession as a buyer and seller of used form machinery. He had all of the paperwork necessary to prove his alias, He had procured the paperwork over the years as an employee of a German cousin's firm in Hamburg. The family connection was on his mother's side, making it virtually impossible to be tracked down to his father's SS lineage, especially since the Kroper name was fictitious, having been coined in Paraguay years after the escape from the Fuhrerbunker.

Kroper had bonded himself to Rosario. Despite his penchant for violence, he was keen minded and appreciated Rosario's similar interest. Kroper's German instinct told him Rosario was clearly a Jew and, therefore, his purported enemy. Indeed, his father had spent years indoctrinating him as a youth that the Jews themselves were to blame for Hitler's power. It was the weak Jews who had failed to stand up to Hitler with all of their money and disproportionate power, going instead like lemmings to their demise, only praying and beating their breasts. There had been only a few noteworthy exceptions, such as Jewish partisans, mostly in France and in Poland at the Warsaw ghetto.

Kroper had seen Rosario save money, a good man in his own companies. He had seen Rosario fight tooth and nail when overrun in combat, taking life just like the other men. Jew or not, he was worthy of respect, and when called upon, Kroger gave Rosario the respect he was due.

A man's history was a forbidden topic in the legion, unless the legionnaire himself brought it up. Only those who weren't hiding in the ranks would venture to do so. They were likely to be lesser men convicted of petty crimes who were prone to drink and do drugs, seeking some concept of adventure. They preferred the company of other such men and were more effective as members of a gang, no longer feeling isolated or alone. In the States, they would most likely have become gang bikers.

No one knew anything to speak of about François "Frenchy" Bastrique's history. They knew where he had been, because his battle decorations and his soldiering abilities told them something. His decorations included Vietnam but not until the late '60s well after Dien Bien Phu forced out the French colonists.

No one knew really what he did. He had no company of men, didn't train with them, or board down among them. He was an inner office man, always to be found wherever there was a command headquarters. Whatever he did, he must have been good at it, since he had risen to be a full colonel just below the rank of general as an enlisted man. By comparison to other armies, the legion has a far sparser upper echelon of superior officers, and Frenchy's rank was an obvious barometer of his success.

He was a small man who looked almost sickly and of pale complexion. He stood only five feet four inches with gray hair. He was quite old for active duty, being well over sixty. Others would hardly expect him to be a blood-and-guts legionnaire, raised up through the enlisted ranks. However, there was no career path. The legion had no Reserve Officer's Training Corps or cadet college. Men started at the bottom and made their way up or not.

The truth was that Frenchy was an intelligence specialist right from the start. He had the ability to understand enemy movements—what was a real and what a false maneuvering ploy. He was a watcher. He could follow a step behind someone, and he wouldn't know it. He was a master of disguise and projected harmlessness and passivity completely dishonestly. He was anything but someone to be ignored, but invariably he was ignored, with few exceptions.

One bad episode had been a surveillance detail gone sour in Barcelona. He had been detailed to a KGB agent, gathering information from various sources about NATO movements. He had been France's contribution to the tracking of the Russians and their informants. He had made no mistakes. He was denounced by another agent, turned informant, in a honey trap during a tryst with a male companion.

Frenchy and three others were exposed. Two were murdered after interrogation; one (an Englishman) had escaped leaving his captors behind and dead. Frenchy had been left for dead, and nearly was by the time he was liberated by the Englishman and taken to a new safehouse outside Barcelona. The Englishman barely kept him alive awaiting help and unable to go to a hospital or the police.

Then the legion mustered Rosario up from his month's leave in Switzerland and jetted him into Spain to a United States air force base without customs entry, moving him by private ambulance to the safehouse. He operated on Frenchy twice and stood by him for three weeks, providing medicines as well as changing bandages and feeding tubes. Finally, Frenchy was moved back to France for six months of recovery and physical therapy. Frenchy owed Rosario his life.

When he was called from Mississippi, he gave notice of leave. He flew Air France to Kennedy and American to Atlanta. He rented a car, driving to New Orleans for an unscheduled rental drop off. He bought a car for cash but used only temporary plates, for which he had twenty days with the title in hand. It was a ten-year-old Ford Econoline 250 van that had cost only a few thousand dollars, including the temporary paper license. Then he all but disappeared. His background told him he could not be found, especially if the van was gone as well. It disappeared two days after he reached Jackson and was settling to the bottom of a manmade lake in an abandoned stone quarry that would never be drained for mining again. It was gone and so was he.

Frenchy had plenty of other IDs stocked away in his travel kit, gathered and used over the years. After all, that was his business. He knew the cameras would never discover his real form and face, which he had wigged and mustached and altered with makeup so many times before with success. He had also gained three inches in the elevated boots he wore for traveling, which were far too uncomfortable for use day in, day out. He had thrown them away in Atlanta, one boot at a time. He bunked down to wait out another day at a Motel Six on the Jackson-Canton Highway before the day four reunion.

Louis Du Preis was an enlisted man. He had never climbed up into the officer ranks and had made staff sergeant only after twenty years in. He had been a small arms expert, a brawler, and a locksmith on the run before joining the legion. His talents were not unique in the legion, but they were well developed. No one so far had beaten him to the punch, which was a significant distinction in the legion, considering the vast number of sucker punch artists to be found in the ranks. He fought for his battalion in boxing exhibitions in the heavyweight class. He stood six feet one inch and weighed about 190 pounds of daily trained muscle, and those exhibitions were about all he did now. At age forty-four, he should have been long over the hill, with so many fights behind him.

Since he was officially still in the legion but living at home and training for five hours daily, he really had no one to ask for leave when Rosario called. He was on his own with no wife or children to announce his departure to. He did have several girlfriends at the time (three actually), but the Gaelic male ego in him did not make it necessary for him to give them any accounting of his whereabouts. If he made it back and they were still around and interested, so much the better. If not, it wasn't important, at least not to him. "Easy come, easy go" was his attitude.

So what did he owe Rosario, he wondered. Nothing really but peace of mind. Six years before, Rosario had been his fight doctor at a championship bout when he was put up against a French Canadian air force kid who had been his sparring partner a year or two before in an intramural national French speaking military competition. The kid and he had bonded, and he had taught him what he could. The kid was okay—a solid puncher—but always a little slow. Worst of all to Louis's mind, he was a telegrapher.

Maybe no one else saw it, but the kid always announced in advance through his bobs which way he was going to throw and when. No way could he outmaneuver Louis and lay him out. Louis saw him coming ten times out of ten.

The fight had gone off in Montreal, and Louis and Rosario had been flown in by military transport from a legion base in Algeria. It was the final and most important bout of the evening, because it was in the heavyweight class. Louis still woke up many years later, drenched in sweat from reliving the fight. He came awake time and again, bemoaning to himself that they should never have put the kid up against him.

The fight was a five rounder. The kid never made three. Louis wanted to take him out early so he could minimize the harm to the kid. He beat at him hard and good in round one. The kid was still a telegrapher, and Louis knew just where he would be. Louis was giving him all head shots, hoping to tire him out quickly and drop him for the count. He was younger then and not really paying attention to the damage he was doing with one head shot after another. The kid was already bleeding from cuts to an eyebrow and his lip at the end of round one. The referee checked him but did not stop the fight. At the opening of the second round, the kid took a teeth-rattling uppercut to the chin followed by two direct face hits from Louis's head. He was bobbing like a rear-deck car puppet on a spring. The fourth shot was a haymaker from down near Louis's right leg—*bang*—into the kid's left temple, collapsing him and ending his boxing career and very likely his life.

The ring master came in, declaring Louis the victor on his wireless microphone, but the champion was paying him no attention. His gloves were already off, and he was opening his strings with his teeth. He lifted the kid up, handing him over the ropes to Rosario, like a child picking up a runover puppy, even with that same look in his wet eyes. Despite the kid's good size, Rosario rushed him to the medical recovery suite.

God bless the Canadians, Louis thought. *They were far cleverer than the French. No way could you do battle without a mandatory medical facility in place, even if it was almost never used.* The Canadians were not banking on any lifesaving ambulance rides to the nearest hospital. No way. All the ringside trainers and doctors also had to view the facility and know its location and equipment, signing off on the same as acceptable before their fighters could weigh in and get approved for a fight.

Rosario ran the kid into the operating room, calling for a portable x-ray unit to try to calculate the damage. There was no MRI equipment on site. When he entered the operating room, it was already staffed with a nurse and a technician on standby and ready because of closed-circuit cameras. They spoke both French and English medically.

The spot film showed swelling in the brain but no skull breaks. The left eye was gone; the swelling was on that side. Rosario scrubbed in and went to work. Louis never made it in. He got shot up with twenty milligrams of valium by a friendly nurse who was a nun. He was escorted to the showers to calm himself down. He got another ten milligrams after the shower and was bedded down, but he did not sleep.

Rosario triaged the kid. He removed and cleaned up the eye, wondering if he should drain the kid through the socket. He was no brain surgeon, but he had been inside the head with his steel tools many times before with battlefield injuries. He took three more scans ten minutes apart, trying to calculate the growth of the swellings of fluid. Thinking he had gotten it but not knowing, he went for the gold, he drilled an opening a half inch behind the left ear meridian. The fluid drained out, and the pressure released. He bandaged the kid, who was transported by medevac helicopter from the arena to a neurosurgery unit at a specialized trauma facility.

Rosario visited with Louis, laying it all out for him.

The kid lost the eye and walked with a slight imbalance. The drainage hole was closed three weeks later by the new doctors. The kid's mental facilities were not impaired. He was fully pensioned out of the service and never fought again. He became a landscape painter, but he never enjoyed commercial success. He married and raised two children. He never spoke with Louis again. He never thanked Rosario, so Louis owed him some thank-you. He owed him the kid's life.

Louis knew he was a keeper of the arms. Rosario was calling him in but had not needed to tell him to bring along the hardware. He never traveled without seeing to arms, if it was for a detail. Louis had no idea what they would need. He had two choices: send it along or buy it stateside. He knew that buying it stateside would be less risky due to customs, even if he used a blind shipment outside his own travel. Moving the goods inside the States was the same level of risk. Buying them there was far more expensive but much safer.

He called an old friend in the Albany area and wired him twenty-five thousand dollars to a Cayman Island bank account. He had paid an extra five thousand. No shopping lists were discussed. If more was needed it would be paid. The extra money was for delivery. No location was stated. He would see the man a day and a half later in Newark, New Jersey.

That would give him two days to get to Mississippi, and the weapons could come after he had learned the score. There was no hurry. He packed with a wary smile on his face, happy to be able to repay Rosario for saving the kid's life.

They should never have put the kid up against me—he thought the neverending mantra yet again.

CHAPTER ELEVEN

All Ye, All Ye "Outs" in Free

It was like the childhood game of ring-a-levio that Rosario had played stateside when he visited his mother's parents in the summer on Cape Cod. Time came the fourth day for all to come home, free and uncaught. He had no doubt that his friends would make it in. They were each professionals in what they did, and avoiding their self-exposure was key to survival. No. They would make it in all right. It had just taken some patient waiting, but four days' time was little enough dues to pay for their help until the job was done.

He had also been busy, even if not traveling in. He had begun to assemble what was needed to start their operation. He had read the local newspapers for property listings, knowing the men would have to stay locally but not with him at the same hotel. To be effective, they would need to keep their distance from him and from each other in public so they would not be linked up together. It would not be long before whomever he was looking for would be looking for him. He would not expose his A-team to their scrutiny or harm.

He had also been dwelling on what Julie had told him: a good bar and restaurant. He looked for these in the real estate business sections and also on the Internet. There were a lot of homes and farmettes available on various sizes of tracts of land, but there very few downtown Jackson bar/restaurants that were not just beaneries and much too small for his purposes. He wanted big, even oversize, and flashy. He also wanted living quarters above the bar/restaurant for staff and himself that could hold his men when the time came. He had had no such luck so far. He didn't want to be too long about it, so it was time to get on with it, see it through to a conclusion.

Day four came early for him. He was up at six a.m., his body still trained to prison time. He showered, shaved, and dressed in casual clothes that he had bought day three from Mr. Goldstien, paying him another visit and letting himself be guided by what the old man thought proper attire for a local businessman. It was mostly banlon shirts and khaki trousers with light socks and ankle-high half boots. A dark blue cotton windbreaker would take care of the early hours and late nights, but so far there had been none.

That morning Rosario had ventured out to the concierge desk. He did not know Julie's schedule—only that she had not worked the two days since they had met. He knew that she would show up, but he was pleased to see her on the early shift as he went for coffee. She gave him a nice smile and a pleasant hello, handing him a black coffee.

"Black, right?" she asked.

Rosario answered with a polite, "Thank you." He asked her if she could sit a minute, and she nodded yes, looking around to note that there were no other guests to occupy her. "I've been thinking about what you said. A bar/restaurant is a good idea. There is not much available in downtown, and that is where I think I should be. The outskirts of Jackson will not draw a good crowd, and drinking while traveling far is not a good idea. I think most of the people would be able to make it home hassle-free from downtown—call a cab or even use a valet service we can provide with college students. We can take cars home too, if need be, for a slight extra charge or keep it overnight. What do you think, Julie?"

"Well, I already told you a bar/restaurant would be the idea. It will probably soon enough show you a good return on your money. I agree downtown is where to be, and college kids to get people safely home just spreads the wealth and makes your bar unique. It appeases the MADD mothers too. Most people down here are hard drinkers, but they have come to fear a DWI stop and the teetotalers who sit at the bar and wait for you to leave tipsy and then call the police on their cell phones, turning you in. Now the police run a nightly roving detail for drunk drivers and are busy. Helping to avoid the problem would relieve you of the MADD crowd pushing people on to the other bars that do not have any such safety plan. Word gets around quick here, Mr. Baloute, and it would make your establishment quite popular and actually upper class. It will also help to keep out the ordinary redneck drunks who are not going to pay top dollar for their alcohol or a courtesy car.

"I think you are not going to find what you need already in place. The bar/restaurants downtown are too small and mostly only watering holes. No dance floors or spacious rooms exist. There are a few good places with quality food, but they are much too small with only ten or twelve tables, and once prosperous, they are not for sale. They might be later if you capture their crowds, but they are still too small. Also the cooking is down-home, and you can get that anywhere, including a BYO establishment.

"A lot of regular folks here like to bring their own and spare the bar bill. They are not your easy money crowd, which does exist. Mostly now, they go to their country clubs or have roving chefs who put up meals on the weekends at various homes for the same old group of friends who rotate hosting. You call in what you want to eat or any special dietary needs. These people have money and really no place to go that suits them. They are mostly the professionals and businessmen who keep their own company and don't mix well with ordinary folk. They don't want to. The higher the prices, the more likely you are to see them."

"It seems you have given a lot of thought to this, Julie. How come?"

"Well, a girl can't just sit around at home, waiting for good luck to just drop success in her lap. Restaurants are gender free. A woman can own a top place as easily as a man. People want the top fare and don't care who gives it to them. For food and drink, they will travel almost any distance. Make it hard to get in, and they flock to the door. They have to be seen and able to talk about it the next day after being at the scene. It's been a thought in my mind for a while, especially here in Jackson where I know there is a void. You don't need a degree from Cornell in restaurant management to know your town is dead."

Rosario had no idea what any upstate New York university had to do with it. He let it pass, already confirmed in his mind that she had indeed given it a lot of thought. Actually, she had given it well more than he had and with far better insight. It was like getting a natural straight on the first deal. A few innocent questions put to a total stranger casually had begotten a virtual game plan for him of what to do. He knew now that a deal with her was in order. He needed not know the why of it. *Make a deal if you can,* he thought. *Use the money carrot if need be.* The money was no risk to him. He had to put it to work and grease the wheel with it, if he wanted to get what he needed.

"Listen, Julie, I have an idea. A proposal really. Don't say yes or no now, because either one would be without your thinking. That's not what I want. If you like it, give me a business plan of your own. What you would want and not what you think would please me. If it makes sense, then it's on. You will manage it, develop it, and help make it work. I will give you the parameters of what I think. Adjust yours as you think thereafter. I pay the freight of purchase and development. You run the show out front for the people. I hang around, watching my investment. If it prospers, we all make out. If it fails, I waste some money but still own the property to cut my losses. Tell me what you think is fair. I will give you a contract for three years' salary win or lose before, so it can make sense for you to commit to the project.

"We will talk again in a few days," he said finally and stood, moving to the elevator bank.

It would have been proper for her to rise, with her still being in service, but her mind was ablaze with ideas and, really, nonbelief. She hadn't even yet taken a few steps on her own to network out of her concierge day job. Some of the girls at college had told her when she started taking fill-in shifts that she might meet a prince charming at the hotel. She had never thought about it really, because she had no desire to dig for gold. She wanted to make it on her own brains and talent. She was confident that she enjoyed such resources but lacked the means—a lot of money—to make it all happen. Short of winning a lottery, it was never going to happen for her! Yet a rainbow had perhaps just dropped a leprechaun in her lap.

There were all sorts of women, both good and wicked, which she knew firsthand. Although she was not Little Miss Innocent, she had never exploited men. She took as hard as she gave in her personal relationships. She didn't know this guy; she knew absolutely nothing about him, and so far, he wasn't saying. True, there had been no come-ons to her as a woman. He seemed truthful in voice and demeanor, but so had John Wayne Gacy when murdering his victims.

If Mr. Rosario was such a big deal, why was he fiddling away in backwater Jackson, Mississippi, even assuming he was a man of substantial means? On the other hand, what could he expect to extract from her? Except for a good night's stand, she had nothing to steal. It brought the old joke about the priest to mind, and she smiled. It was her own dilemma. She thought it out to see if it had an answer but no, it was only a joke about an old priest who had left the church after a midday celebration of the faith hand-in-hand with a young boy. A parishioner outside had spied him and thought the worst. He started coming up behind them, quickly coming closer and closer. Suddenly, the priest turned on his heels confronting his shadow.

"Amos, Amos, I never knew. Would you like to fuck the little boy, too?"

Amos was shocked by the priest's candor. He paused for only a few seconds.

"Fuck him out of what, father?"

That was the issue. How could this stranger pull one over on her? Time would tell. It would be better to get to it sooner rather than later. She needed to figure out what he wanted: a plan for business. It sure seemed like a proper approach. She set her mind to it, making and changing notes on a pad while letting her fantasies run a little wild. What bells and whistles would she want? Money was not the object. Maybe there should be a theme like a Disney park of Graceland?

Rosario was pleased. He had moved his game plan forward. Maybe she was as smart as she looked, maybe not. Time would tell. He would give her a fair shot at it and see what she came up with. Whatever it cost, he could well afford it. It would be pretty funny if it was a business success. What he needed it to do was only to bring in the prey, to see them firsthand and help them to reveal themselves and set the stage for payback.

One genuine problem still existed. The whole point of it was simple. He had to create a local presence in his own identity. He could not hide behind it. He had no background to judge how it would play out. Would customers boycott it because a convicted criminal was behind it? Would putting Julie out front save the day? Would they turn the other cheek and flock to it as Julie predicted? Would there not certainly be at least some substantial controversy? No one had these answers, and so there was no choice but to move forward and find out.

He left the hotel lobby at 7:35 a.m. Jackson was awake. The downtown people were already on the move, going to their jobs, coming off the busses, or racking up the early morning parking specials. He was on the streets less than a minute before he saw Frenchy. He didn't need a double take. He could almost smell his presence. He had known that he would be the first one in.

Frenchy didn't look like a vagrant. He just didn't look prosperous. He was wearing jeans with rolled cuffs and a well-worn, woolen, red plaid shirt like a laborer. He had a sweat bandana tied around his neck and a tarnished blue North Carolina State baseball cap. Rosario could not see his face well, because the cap hid his features. If he took it off, lowered the pants, and ditched the neckwear, he would be hard to spot even moments later. Rosario was sure the oversize plastic bag Frenchy carried held more disguise.

He wandered on in Frenchy's direction, the only one of the two moving. Frenchy held his spot, waiting for the bump and drop. He was partway turned away when Rosario reached him on the sidewalk. Frenchy turned into him excusing himself loudly and stumbled a bit himself, moving forward and away. Anyone looking would have thought it an accident and not a rehearsed movement. No one saw the paper folded in Rosario's left hand, protruding two inches out from his fisted fore and middle finger knuckles. No one saw Frenchy seize it deftly, secreting it out of sight in his left hand. It was too quick and too soon begun and finished. Anyone looking would have just seen the bump and heard the apology at best.

The message was brief. It too was practiced. The paper was a gum wrapper with the writing on its inside. It read "C16Sp4W" and nothing more.

French people were invariably Catholic. Chaplains in the legion were Catholic—not Proddies or Jews or, certainly, Mussies. If men wanted to pray, they did it Catholic. Men died and got the last rites, whether Catholic or not. God would sort them out, not the legionnaire chaplains. The legion had its own rules for the dead or dying.

C was invariably "church" and was mostly unnecessary. A majority of undercover secret rendezvous took place in churches. The reason was simple but had manifold purposes. If someone following was not Catholic, he would soon reveal himself inside by failing to bow and scrape at the proper places or during mass by sitting too long and not rising or by failing to cross himself or speak in participation. Followers were trained to know their limitations, so they might not enter the church and simply wait for the subject to exit, therefore not revealing himself inside. However, a careful target would notice him beforehand and after by the walk or by noting that his appearance had changed but not the shoes. Thus, exposure was revealed by the hiatus if someone's tradecraft training had been productive enough to hone his observation skills. It was six of one or a half dozen of the other whether to risk venturing into church or not, but most usually not, because it led to being plainly spotted, especially if there was any hookup by others newly joining in the rendezvous. If the follower got spotted, he risked not only exposure and so failure but also harm. There were likely others who might take him out. So a large capital *C* meant "church."

Meetings locations were followed by times. "16" was four p.m. in military time. That was easy if someone knew it but puzzling, at least for a while, if he did not. It could be a street number or even a phone reference or a person's ID number. "16" alone was not clear sailing. And if it was a time, was the ending "4" an alteration for adding, subtracting, dividing, or the like for any meeting time?

Churches have names. "SP" was Saint Patrick and not Saint Paul or

Saint Peter. They all had their own short hand. "P" was Paul. "PS" was Saint Peter. The "4" actually meant that Frenchy was to round up the other two, having them make their own way into the meeting, each seeing that the others were clean coming in. The last man in was to make sure the others were clean.

"W" was wheels. Someone was to have a car for four standing by. This would let them lose any followers who lacked ready car access. "F" would mean foot, so no car backup would be necessary. "W" further means car and not horse, buggy, or anything else, at least in the legion. There was an old legion joke about a not-too-bright legionnaire who was summoned into a "W" meeting in Lyons on an espionage detail. It was a three-man meeting. He came on a motorcycle with two helmets. Out went the three from church, and the lead man spotted the problem. He and the other comrade took off on the bike, leaving its owner stranded. The police had been observing as followers, but there was little they could do when the story was that the twosome of interest had stolen his bike. The third could not be held long, and he was let go four days later when the trail of his buddies went cold. He did get payback. His new but permanent nickname for the rest of his tours was "Wheels."

CHAPTER TWELVE
Follow-Up

Rosario's day was hardly started, but now it was already half over. Contact had been made, and the meeting was set for eight hours hence. Part one was over. There was not much to do and no reason to linger around.

He stepped into a small corner drugstore of substantial vintage, proclaiming 110 years at the same location and still operated by the Clayton family. He bought local newspapers and left. He had free ones in his concierge floor common room, but he thought it would be impolite and even cheap-minded to take them to his room. The purchase was also a way to cool down the bump if anyone had picked up no it, which he very much doubted. It was too soon for watchers and for his whereabouts to be an issue.

When he was back upstairs, his floor was still unoccupied. If it was to fill up, it would likely be by tonight, as the weekend was upon them. So far there had been no early check-ins. He wasn't going to confront Julie. It was simply too soon, and he was not expecting a reply yet. He was wrong.

"I've been thinking about it while you were gone. You must know what you need at a minimum. You might as well fill me in, and I can give you what I think just to open the discussion."

"Julie, I think I want a several-story building with fifteen thousand to twenty thousand square feet for ground floor space. That way I can have an adequate-size kitchen and barroom and enough space for several different styles of entertainment areas with a few private dining rooms. The upper floors could hold staff quarters, a gym for their use, training areas, and on the top floor, I would keep my own apartment so I would always be onsite. An elevator would be ideal, as would a basement for storage, food lockers, and an eating area for the staff. I don't need garages, but off-street parking is a must. I think we should have valet service at the front door. I don't see doing lunch. I want it to be exclusive so at full price and not disconnected by any midday meal. It's not worth it in my mind. Actually, I might not even open until seven p.m. to let the executives get home, have a drink, change their workday clothes, shower, relax a little, kiss the kids, and grab the wife or whomever. It's much better to come to dinner than to have them just wander in still uptight from the office. There will also be regulars, and we can let them in a little earlier, giving them some distinction of preference. What do you think?"

"I understand it all, but I need to dwell some more on it. The location will be the hard part. There is certainly no place now with that much ground space, let alone the upper stories. You will have to build it out."

"If I do, then I can. No problem, except I would like to skip the time that takes. I don't want to spend a year just getting open. Have you any thoughts about what you need to come on board?"

"Yes. I think a three-year arrangement is proper. It's not too long and not too short to get it done, so it works, especially if we have to resolve a menu, the themes, and draw a proper crowd should the unforeseen arise. After all, Rosario, you are a stranger, and Mississippi people are not that keen on you if you are not born and bred here. I am sure you know this."

"Well, there is an issue there, Julie, which we need to discuss. First, let me hear your side in full, please."

"I think a salary of one thousand dollars a week would be proper. I did not yet consider the aspect of living onsite as to the cost of room and board. If it works and we are both happy going forward, I should have an option to purchase ten percent of the business at a price we fix now, so I can buy myself a lifetime opportunity. Is that a problem?"

"Julie, I am more focused on success than I am on money. If it works, we should all prosper. I am not given to arguing over money. I want to end those topics at the beginning. I think your proposal is fair, but it shorts you in the long run. I don't expect to be at this forever. Within three years or less, I will likely move on to other opportunities. You will be left behind to carry the football alone. You work, but I prosper too, even absentee if I choose to go elsewhere. Therefore, to start, I would say one thousand five hundred dollars a week for the first three years, and at the end of this, I will give you twenty percent ownership. You can go too or stay to make it pay off even better. Up to you. These are simple details. I can put the stock up at the beginning if you wish. Deal?"

"Deal." She came back, rising to shake his extended hand. There was still a distance between them, so there was no hugging or cheek petting, just hand shaking, eyeball to eyeball with both of them pretty serious.

"You were going to tell me something now?"

"You'll hear it sooner or later, and it is an obstacle we need to get around by good planning at the outset. We need to make certain as best we can that there are no stumbling blocks and, if there are, plan how to chisel them down. No doubt your presence might help, given your local presence for years, even as an outsider initially. I think, however, if people see it more as your place than mine, it will help. Actually, I don't want someone from here. It's too local. You never know how long they will stay in favor. I believe, if we give the people what they want, they will party in. Old stories won't matter, if we give these people what they want. We know that no one else has so far. We show them a really good time, show them top goods for top dollar."

"I can't say much about that, Rosario, until I know what problem exists and think about how to get around it."

The ground had been broken between them, and they both knew it. They were talking about "we," and she was calling him Rosario. They were beginning to bond. Now it was down to the details, assuming that being convicted of three murders could be just that—a detail. *If it is*, Rosario thought to himself, *then it is sure one hell of a detail and not some little bitty thing*. It could turn her (or anyone else for that matter) off at the start. Now was the time to find out.

"A year ago last fall, there was the triple church murder. It was on the first day I arrived from France. I was the one they scooped up and tried and sent to jail. I just got out with good time."

"I remember it. It was all over town. A lot of people were very upset by it. Still are. It was the body carving that got them, along with the murder of the children! Most people think that they tried the wrong person. That means a lunatic is still on the loose, and folks sure are still waiting for 'Werewolves of London' to strike again. Others say that, because there was nothing more, they got the right man."

"Well, they didn't, Julie. Only a few people, and not the public, know that I am free. I did my time. I am not going to run and hide. I need to set the record straight now and forever before I can go on my way with any peace of mind."

"Sure, you do, or you would already be long gone. It's why you need to stick it out here and open a showplace."

"Is that a problem for you, Julie?"

"Not hardly. Since we are being open, Rosario, and doing a little show-and-tell, I'm not from a hick background in Michigan. My father is a lawyer, a criminal lawyer … a former county prosecutor made good who taught his children not to judge. I learned many innocent people get convicted and a lot of guilty ones go free. It's the way the system works. It has little to do with guilt or innocence. The state will convict you if it can."

"No doubt about that, Julie."

"Actually, Rosario, in the end, you probably won even if it cost you time and freedom. Judge Stittin actually cleared you. He made it plain he did not believe it. He is not exactly a local boy, but given his marriage, in a way he is. No one else is trusted with the heavy capital cases. He married well into a local family of distinct enough influence to see him. His word means a lot. Cutting you slack in sentencing made it plain what happened. If he had cut you loose, it would not have worked. The state would appeal, and you would be retried and convicted on retrial in another court. You'd probably get life or close to it. Can't do it now."

"So what do you think the harm potential is to our project, Julie?"

"No way to tell, Rosario. I guess if the Southerners and their friends join our crowd, it would be damage control. But there is no real way of telling in the abstract up front. You just have to wait and see or quit now."

"I am not stopping yet, not quitting even before the water gets rough. Let me know in a day or two if you are in or out."

"I am no schoolgirl, Rosario. Twenty to eighty percent is not the difference. Going in, we are equals in energy to see it work. I'm in, and we can give it our best shot, work our way around it as best we can, if we can. Let's give the crowd what they want and hope that does the job. I agree that there is no sense hiding. You paid your dues. Time to get on with it."

"Any other questions, Julie?"

"Sure, there are questions, Rosario. Who are you really? What's the game plan? Whose money is it? Why? But this is still not my business. Let me know if and when they are. Deal?"

"Deal," he said and got up to go to his room. It was time to shower and get ready for church. There really was nothing else to talk about. Discussions were over. It was time to move forward.

CHAPTER THIRTEEN
Meeting Up

Rosario was watching the front door of Saint Patrick's Roman Catholic Church on Commerce Street in downtown Jackson. It was actually a cathedral, although its façade had become worn over the decades. It needed a good sandblasting to clean the effects of sun and acid rain. The church had been built in the '30s when religion was in its heyday. Its congregation had been in decline since the late 1950s, when Catholicism went suburban, with people migrating from the center city, learning to pray there and eat at strip malls and shop at their large fashionable anchor stores. Oversize food stores could cut the prices on volume sales and smaller size, hip, pocket churches could do the reverse, making do with much smaller congregations. Inner city had been dying ever since the Exodus.

The cathedral would have closed years before but for the fact that the bishop of Mississippi was lodged there, which made it the center of the state's dioceses. The cathedral was still well populated with clergy (both priests and nuns) who staffed its parochial school, which still provided a far superior education. The prices were high, but the education and results remained superb. Many Protestant and other religious families sent their children to school there, and the boarding facility held nearly a hundred boarders, mostly from Catholic families, from many of the other Southern states. Many of the children were committed in the old style to join the clergy. That meant the cathedral was always busy with sports competitions, conferences, community events, weddings, funerals, and other church events needed to sustain their congregation.

For this reason, many people went in and out of the church on a steady basis when Rosario took up his surveillance post early. The church itself sat on six acres with a more modern rectory, a mother house, and ancillary buildings for the administration of the school and other events. The school and its dormitories for students and priests were actually located in the suburbs, having outgrown the downtown facility long before. There was private bus service between the two from early in the day to nine at night. The church was also an attraction for Catholics visiting Jackson as a must-see, and daily services were invariably well attended.

None of the hustle and bustle in and out of the front door was distracting. Rosario spotted his friends coming in from a distance. These men had warred, bunked, ate, fought, and whored together. They were blood-bonded by choice. There was no missing them, even when they were disguised for others. Rosario watched them to try to detect any followers. He saw none. He noted Frenchy, who had gathered the others up, came in first and waited for the other two to pass him; he was also trying to pick up anyone on their tails. He saw none either. It was still too soon for company. The followers would come later.

Frenchy was last man in. Rosario passed him by, letting him know that he, too, had been watching. It was all clear, with Frenchy bringing up the rear. By 4:10 p.m., they were all seated in the rear pew at the main altar. The afternoon four o'clock mass was in progress. At 4:25 p.m., when communion was offered, Frenchy stood with the congregation, moving to line up. The other men did likewise. He dropped a bill in the collection basket and left by the exit by the side alter, moving slowly away to a rectory parking lot. He entered a dirty, gray, six-year-old Ford 350 diesel pickup with a four-door passenger cab. He started up the oversize V8. The other men followed him out and entered the vehicle. Frenchy backed out, moving away slowly and removing a sign that said "Clergy" from the front window and then taking State Street to head out of downtown.

With the doors locked and the windows tinted against the strong

Mississippi sun, the men were settling down. The greetings and joking and backslapping had begun. It was legionnaire behavior, and the initial tension level was covered by the gay reunion in progress. The men were joking with each other about the effects of the passage of time on their appearances. None but Rosario knew why they were together, but that would come later. It was time for a little fun.

Rosario was in the rear passenger seat, just about fully settled in, when Frenchy shot him a "Where to?" Rosario knew where he wanted to go, but he was not sure how to get there. He had ripped the local map out of the phone book in his room and studied it. He knew they called it only the "diner" or the "airport diner" but no other name. No such place was listed in either the White or Yellow Pages.

The map told him pretty much which roads he had hiked from the airport, but he could no longer remember any twists or turns in the roads he had taken more than a year before. He knew that the church was on the same road, even if farther up, and he tracked it down to Citizens Highway, knowing the diner must be on it. He marked it where he thought it should be.

"Not sure, Frenchy, but *X* marks the spot," he said, handing the map forward. It was the best he could do without asking Julie to Mapquest the church. There was no sense including her yet.

Frenchy slowed nearly two miles later at a major intersection, pulling to a stop while the other men were still getting caught up, teasing and joking each other about times and events of yesteryear. Frenchy studied the street signs, the map, and the *X* and tried to figure the distances, not knowing if the map had any scale to its design. He set off again, driving slowly and using his turn signals. He had always been a born wheelman and did nothing erratic to call attention to his driving. Minutes later with a fair amount of maneuvering and doubling back but without checking the map again, he thought he had it spotted.

"Tell me what you think, Doc. It's on the right if you were coming from the airport. We are coming in from the other side."

Frenchy had figured out Rosario had been walking south after eating before bunking down in darkness. Rosario had told him nothing about it except the most superficial map details. In the hiatus waiting out their rendezvous, Frenchy had figured it out on his own and read up on it in the local newspapers from arrest to trial, conviction, and Judge Stittin's utterances.

As they passed it moving slowly, Rosario was able to study it. No doubt about it, it was the diner all right. Rosario wasn't ready to study the church yet. He told Frenchy to reverse and pull into the diner. The men, now quiet, moved into the eatery slowly, with Rosario going in first.

Empty wasn't the word. There were no customers, three servers, and an inside kitchen cook behind the counter, counting the register. It was only a year later, but Rosario was sure he had never seen any of them before. Certainly, little miss bump-and-tell Vickie Trucker was not about. He hadn't expected her to be. The waitress who had served him wasn't about either. Those who were there were older and heavier and looked particularly less friendly. They were all strangers. There was no good old group greeting but instead just one hello. One server told the others she had the next group and showed them to her table, putting the menus down. All she got back was a hello in unison from four of them in accent-free English.

She got the water. They picked up the menus. She asked about coffee and got four yeses or "Pleases." They got the coffees and a crème pitcher; she got four orders for eggs and bacon with toast. There was not much excitement on either side. The other three diner workers just looked on, paying no real attention when the men had all ordered diner food, which was "breakfast all day long."

The food came. The men ate. The coffee flowed and no one said very much except about the ketchup, sugar bowl, or cream. It was Rosario's show. He would set the level of talking. The server offered pies, rice and bread pudding, and three types of cakes. She got two apple pie orders. Rosario asked for the check and handed her a fifty dollar bill on less than a forty-dollar check, leaving the change down. They all got refills. She got to sit down and relax at the end of the counter with the others across the room, about as far away as they could get.

Everyone settled in, friends and strangers from both points of view. Rosario got started.

"You all know what happened to me?" He got their nods. Frenchy had told them. "That's why we're here, why I need help to get to the bottom of it. I need to get my reputation back and my life back on one even keel before going back home. I have some ideas about how, but we have time for that. For now, we need a way to do it, so let me tell you what I think. There's no pride in authorship. You see missing details or mistakes, shout up."

The initial tension of meeting had settled down. The men were reunited, fed, and settled in. They listened closely.

"We need everyone mobile—more cars, Frenchy—but nothing to come back to us, if you can. Just let me know how much you need. If we can avoid it, don't register them to us. Make them the old worn paint types the locals drive. Maybe another pickup. Make one of them for me only a few years old, black, upper price range like a businessman would drive. Maybe a big Buick or Chevrolet four-door, as large as you can get. No foreign cars.

"Kroper, we need a house. Here they have what they call 'farmettes,' old farm houses usually with twenty acres or more. The more secluded the better, with a large barn or four garages to put the cars out of sight. A long driveway is best. We can wire it for incoming detection. Some of these places are fenced on either side of the driveway, all the way up to the main house, which is more secure. Horses are easy to let pasture, making it look like a farm, so if it has a horse barn too, it's all the better. The fences will slow anyone down. Some also have a rear way out around the fences back to the main road or out to a back road. A back road can be also a way in so I don't want that."

The men were nodding that they were taking it in and just not speaking.

"We are likely to have some unhappy stayover visitors. We need a holding area we can lock down. Price doesn't matter, but the most secure location and how it's fitted out does. No nearby neighbors is best. We need to be only fifteen to twenty minutes out, so we can get in and out of town quickly. It's best if no houses are near the driveway, so we can come and go as we like, unseen. These people—men, women, and children—are all nosey. They have nothing else to do but snoop and pry. The farther away from observation the better."

"Got it, Doc," Kroper spoke up.

"Use a broker, Kroper, to show you. Wherever you are now, move to the Holiday Inn out of town near the hospital up by Primo's. It is easy to come and go—no lobby—and you can park away from the room entrance. It has staircases open at both ends. Use an upper floor, since it's got more choices for coming and going. Stay out of the elevators. Frenchy and Louis, stay where you like but not together. Same rules, and no places with lobbies. For now coordinate with Frenchy and not me, so we keep contact down until we have our safehouse.

"Kroper, tell the broker you came to paint and maybe write a little poetry. No one can ask you to fire off a demonstration. Tell him you are looking to settle in, so the grandchildren can stay with you for a month in the summer. Ask for a year to rent. Tell him you will pay in advance each year, but you want two years at the same rate and, if sold, the right to buy it at the same price. It will make you interesting to the broker. He will get paid on a sale to you. When you find the right place, look at several more and argue with the price a little. Here they all do that. It's not France. It's not impolite. They expect it and set the prices higher to come down. Also, they are getting the rent up front. It gives you leverage. Give them a blind passport, and no one uses a legionnaire name for any reason."

There were more nods from them all. There was no reason to speak up. They would know Rosario had already worked it all out in advance. These were not just simple ideas but a full battle plan.

"On weapons, I'm not sure yet. I knew we paid, but these people are gun crazy. I'm not sure what we need. You think about what you want. I can't be armed here, even as a released criminal, and probably you can't as foreigners. The cars we can outfit with cut-ins for handguns. When we see the house, we can fit in wall armories in the garage, barn, and house. You never know where you will end up. Louis can do the carpenter work easily and cut out the metal work in the cars when we see what we have.

"If anyone wants anything special—shot guns, gas, or grenades—tell Louis, so he will know to outfit it in, okay?"

"Okay," they all said.

"I am thinking of opening a large bar/restaurant. I have a local girl who may help, and she knows my past, but only since I got here. I want to see if she figures you out. I need to see how alert she really is, to see if she speaks up when she thinks she has it, being loyal or not. She knows I'm here to get to the bottom of it. She was not born here, but she has become local by four years of college. So far, money moves her.

"No speaking anything but American English until we have a better idea of her. I don't know if she speaks French or whatever else. Most of these college kids study some other languages or travel enough to pick something up. Trust me, she is smart, but what else we can't yet tell.

"That's it for now, unless you have questions. There's money in the car to get started. If anyone is running low, just let me know. No one on their own … it's my treat all the way. Don't keep expense records, and write nothing else down. We all need cell phones bought by the same person at different places and then prepaid calling cards with a few hundred on each. Louis, pick them up, please. Anybody want anything to go?"

No one spoke up. They stood and left.

"Thank you. Have a blessed day," Rosario said to their server. Southerners in Mississippi, Rosario knew by then, loved a good religious blessing. Giving it showed that someone understood. People fit right in, even if they were strangers. They were not considered Yankees or foreigners, but deep-fried Southern-style Jesus freaks.

They dropped Rosario off three blocks away from his hotel. By then, it was dark. The streets were totally empty, and he made it upstairs, feeling good that they had gotten started. That made him happy, after so much time and trouble, to see old comrades, each committed to whatever would come, all legionnaires to the end. Friends were one thing, and comrades were another, being so much deeper and far more committed, no matter what it took.

The top floor of the hotel had begun to fill up. The concierge room held eleven guests, eating the free snacks and working the two young females on duty. Julie had gone. He said hello, took a cup of coffee, and went to his room to shower.

He called down for a salad and bottled water and waited, thinking out yet more details for moving forward, knowing there were still a lot of blanks to be filled in. He knew he could not even guess how long it would take them, but he was not really concerned about it. Time, money, and good company he had. He was in no hurry and didn't plan to be.

CHAPTER FOURTEEN

Home Sweet Home

The days passed. It turned a little colder, and the days got shorter. It seemed like nothing was happening. But that was not so. The search in the suburbs had at least paid off. After using a broker and seeing nearly twenty properties, one was selected southwest of the city. It fit the bill. They rented it in the manner Rosario had set forth.

It sat on twenty-five acres, most of which were pasture or corn fields. It was a thoroughbred farm that had been owned by a wealthy physician who had kept four race horses, and not as a hobby. His horses routinely had come home in the money, and their owner had been a known heavy better. Over the years, he had done very well, but his children were long since grown and moved away; no one had wanted the farm when he had passed on a few years back. It hadn't sold, so finally they rented it. Rosario's was the only offer, so making the deal was easy.

As they had hoped, the property was fenced in, with training corrals on either side of the half-mile–long gravel driveway going all the way back to the house. The gravel would slow drivers down, raising dust and making noise as the gravel hit the undercarriages of cars. Unless someone had the control device, he couldn't get in unless he called from the front gate posts, asking to have the large steel interlocking gates opened. Crashing through them or the post and rail would be impossible. The fencing was not set every eight to ten feet but every four feet. The posts were eight feet up and four feet in the ground in cement footings. Each cross plank was about fifty pounds of treated oak, sun-bleached and stained only with waterproofing, set a foot apart and rising up eight courses. The only thing missing was barbed wire.

The broker had apologized for all the security, saying that it detracted from the appearance of the homestead. He had showed them how it all worked. The closed circuit system for the whole property was monitored both in the big house and in a bunkhouse built for the trainers and workers. It housed eight and had a full kitchen and showers. There was no way anyone could get in or out without being monitored and detected. The broker told them that the owner had done it in years gone by to prevent watchers from timing the performance of the thoroughbreds' workouts on the full-size one-and-a-half–mile racetrack set well out of sight behind the big house. Although it was not part of the rental, the estate also owned all of the land around the outside, a full twenty-five acres of post and rail to prevent observers who could not otherwise be shut out from spying on the horses' workouts if they owned the land. Secure it was.

The big house had been built in the late 1940s, but it had been fully redone inside with new plumbing, central air conditioning, and backup generators that were able to power the whole property if, for some reason, the solar electricity system failed. The work had been done a few years before the owner had died. The horse barn held ten stalls and was equally modern. The old pull door garage for the farm tractors and haying bailer held room for eight cars and had a workshop for repairs and carpentry. It had automatic remote electric doors for six bays, so people could enter or leave quickly without getting out.

There was a rear exit on a small lane at the rear of the track that was also about a half-mile long. It let out by a nearby stream that they would have to drive along nearly two miles to hit the county road. A four-wheeler was best to use back there, but a car and a good driver could make it. Coming in unwanted was another matter. Someone would have to know the way in and would not know that the cameras picked him up at the rear gate, which was as sturdy as the front one, being chained closed in three places.

The men, including Rosario, all picked their rooms of the six available and set up and stocked the house with fresh linen, clothes, food, drink, bottled water, juices, and medical supplies of every sort. Cleaning and household materials were brought in, but no furniture, radios, or televisions were needed. The house was being rented fully furnished. Rosario would not permit showings during his rental period except in the last two months unless he renewed. The men went to work and personalized it for their use.

Louis had looked the house over to see where to put an armory. He built a false wall gun safe in two small alcoves in the barn and bunkhouse. He wired in an electronic closing device, outfitted with his own magnet-locking design. To get in, they would have to know where to push the two pressure switches simultaneously to cancel the power circuit that controlled the lock. Otherwise, they had to know to kill the circuit breaker and which one.

Louis was looking to do the same in the house. He studies the walls near the rear mudroom by the back door. He measured the false wall to take a spot two feet deep and six foot wide. He had picked the spot, because it was the most logical place with easy access if trouble came quickly. Only then, did he discover how great minds think alike.

The doctor who had lived there had also had his concerns. When Louis measured from the outer wall in to locate his space, he discovered that there was already a shortfall of four feet deep by ten feet wide. When he stood in the basement looking up, there was no explanation with flooring or plumbing. It was covered in dead space sealed by sheet rock to the molding upstairs. He removed the molding all around and left the coat hooks in the false wall. He was able to see in. It was clearly a hiding area. He used a stud finder to locate any metal latches and found two spring pressure switches, which, when pushed together by hand and foot, allowed the sheet rock to open when he pulled a bolted-in coat hook for leverage. The wall safe was a treasure trove of goodies. The doctor had been a gun freak.

CHAPTER FIFTEEN

Down to Business

Julie and he passed in the lounge, always with a good hello or pleasantries at best but nothing of real substance. There were no in-depth discussions of what was happening or when it would bear fruit, if ever. All Julie would say was "Still looking."

It was only a few weeks later, and she had found no place to set their restaurant. It didn't seem to Rosario that she was working all that much on it. If she was, then it was her own mystery. He thought to wait another week and then put it to her, asking what had been going on and what she had been doing.

The question and answer proved unnecessary. Maybe he was prejudiced about people, he thought, or Americans at least. She said she would do it, and he hadn't given her enough credit for being a self-starter.

On a Wednesday morning about three weeks after they shook on their deal, he got a note from her through the bellman when he went through the lobby. She asked to meet around three p.m. on his floor to talk, telling him she was not on shift, so they would not be disturbed. He was to tell the bellman yes or no. So far, they had not talked about how he could reach her. She knew where to find him mostly anytime, so he had left it alone, not putting her under any pressure, letting her set her own pace and knowing she could.

"Tell, Julie, yes, please," he said, giving the bellman a ten dollar bill for his efforts. All he got back was, "Yes, sir."

Rosario wasn't sure if the bellman was repeating the answer or acknowledging the request. He didn't question it further and went out to eat, looking to kill time for nearly four hours until their meeting. He wondered what she needed or had found, if anything.

He had looked at some listings and visited a few of them on his own. All of them, even from the outside, were too small, not properly located (either too far from downtown itself or on a side street without parking on site or conveniently nearby). He had found nothing remotely acceptable, even with major concessions. He had thought it wasn't going to happen, and he might need to think of a better business road to bring the people to him. He was beginning to think of a sports gym or a compromise on just a sports bar with a little food and no dining room or onsite residences. Something was better than nothing.

He was restless to get the search going and not happy to be waiting much longer. It made him just plain itchy. He was a man of action, and being in repose or dependent upon an unknown woman was just plain uncomfortable. Patience was not his virtue and had never been. "Get on with it" was his mantra. Waiting out the jail time, even with the warden's reprieve, had not helped his personality any either. Chilling out was not his thing, and he even found wasting the next few hours waiting arduous.

By two forty-five p.m., he was upstairs in the concierge lounge, coffee in hand. She was out of the elevator by 2:50. He was relieved that the wait was over.

Hellos were exchanged.

She opened, "Rosario, do you want to talk here or in your suite?"

He had not thought about that. It must have something to do with their level of discussion. He agreed that the room would be better—*more private,* he thought—and said so. Making a reversal in the service role, he asked if she would like anything to drink or eat from the concierge floor or downstairs.

"No," was her solitary reply, and it set him thinking that he had never seen her even sneak a grape or a coffee. Most of the concierges he knew from observation fed themselves and friends with take-home from the service kitchen, but not her so far as he could see. Maybe it was a weight thing. He didn't know. It was not his business. It seemed to him just petty and personal, a discussion he didn't want to have at all. He wanted her motivated by good money and to be all business. He intended to buy her loyalty, not to win it on a social basis.

Soon enough, they were all settled in. His suite was comfortable with a sitting room outside of the bedroom area. She knew it. She knew all the rooms and their layouts. He appreciated her discretion for privacy. He opened with, "Well, what have we?," being unable to better steer the topic or delay his anxious interest with chitchat.

"What I think we have, Rosario, is a location solution," she said, putting it in terms that made it clear that any decision was up to him. She did not await comment but continued on, needing to report her full deeds to show him that she had been on it from the start.

"I did my research, seeing what was around. I found a commercial broker—a woman—who is local and has a good reputation. Many of the men are sharks and don't respect women enough to do business. This is especially true as to me since I am not true-blue Mississippi born and bred, and it is obviously going to cost substantial sums of money that they would know I don't have. Grace—Mrs. Grace Trouller—had no trouble with it and did her job. We looked at more than ten properties, but each was unfit—too far or too small or otherwise just no good. By looking with me, she got a better idea of what we needed. She came up with a property that was not listed.

"Grace and her husband are Catholics. She is from an Italian family, and her husband's family is French, but they have been here a hundred years or more. They are involved in the local affairs of the church. Not three blocks from here is a shutdown facility, which has been empty for two years but not listed for sale. The congregation built a new YMCA in the suburbs to cater to the congregation and its children. It's very modern, a real showplace."

Rosario said nothing, knowing now for sure that she had understood the project from the outset and that the full details would be forthcoming. There was no proving needed of her skills.

"The building sits on nearly two acres and is just as you described, being four stories tall with about twenty-four thousand feet, not counting the basement, which holds the power plant and is finished with only concrete that is set to cinderblock walls. The elevator pits are open for service. There is a front passenger elevator for twenty people and one in the rear for freight or about ten people, which can also open to a loading dock with an outside door for deliveries."

He just nodded and said nothing, not wanting to interrupt her description flow. It was clear that she was pleased with her find.

"The money to move to the suburbs came from a donation from a local businessman whose wife died. She was a daily churchgoer, and he gave eight million dollars, but only for a new facility, and the congregation needed to raise the rest. This was five years ago but totally unexpected. Less than ten years ago, with no such gift, the old YMCA built in the 1950s had been fully done over and upgraded. After the new one was built, it was shut down. The church has no use for it, but still has to carry it, paying for a caretaker to cut the grass and paint when needed and paying taxes, since it is not exempt. They would like to get rid of it."

And I would like to buy it reserve, he thought, not yet knowing the price.

"The ground floor has the biggest footprint, and some is on a slab that was built out later. This is mostly kitchen, which was modernized during the renewal, and it is two thousand square feet with another ten thousand square feet on the ground floor. The basement is long and narrow, being a little over three thousand square feet, and each upper floor is about four thousand square feet. The third floor has about twelve bedroom suites, a men's and women's bathroom area, and a separate master suite with its own bathroom.

"The second floor is mostly open space with small bathrooms, toilets, and sinks only. The ceilings are ten feet high and already dropped, and the heating is central furnace heat or air conditioning, with heating units on the ground and air conditioning dropped from the roof. There is an electric sauna for ten on the second floor and a small gym with five pieces of equipment and two TVs in place already. It is mirrored all around."

With such improvements, Rosario didn't think it resembled a church building. Things in frame were different, more secure. It sounded more like a casino.

"The top floor has a bedroom, windowed floor to ceiling facing out on Mississippi Street its whole length, and a modern whirlpool, blue-tiled bathroom that is really quite pretty. The space is able to be easily divided. The whole building is alarmed, but by whom I don't know. The outside has about one hundred fifty lined parking spots with good lighting, as does the building, which has heavy floods on the corners. It needs painting inside, but the outside is all brick, well done, and clean looking. Now for the price."

"Should I be standing up or sitting down, Julie?" Rosario interrupted her monologue, already knowing that this had to be the place.

"Do as you like, Rosario, but there is no liquor license. The church didn't need one for functions, and they were not running a regular bar there. There are several available at different costs if you want to sell package or not."

"'Package?'" he asked.

"'Package' means to go out, so you can sell closed bottled like a liquor store. If you don't need that, you can get a bar-only license for about thirty thousand dollars, but you have to move it from its stated location to yours. It's a lot of paperwork but not denied almost ever, unless it's going to be next to a school or church, which is not a problem here. A convicted felon can't own the liquor license, Rosario, so you will need a nominee. You can, however, lend the money, so you can take a lender's interest in it until repaid, just like a bank, so you won't risk losing it if problems arise."

"No problem, Julie. You can own it, right? Even in Mississippi, a woman can own a bar, I would think." He smiled at his small joke. So did she.

"Teasing me, Rosario? Making your first joke so far?" *Loosening up maybe,* she thought.

"Yes, unless you are really from Mississippi, Julie," he said with a broad grin that finally relaxed them both. "Please ask Grace to put together a contract and make a formal offer."

"Rosario, you haven't even heard the price."

"I don't need to, Julie. I know it's not more than a hundred dollars a square foot, and I can easily afford that, but down here it must be much less. This isn't Los Angeles or New York, and they want out. Okay, how much?"

"Grace said, all things considered and based on what she had heard given the upkeep savings, it could be it would go for about two hundred fifty thousand dollars—all cash—to get rid of it. More, if you want a mortgage back. She is pretty sure, because this is the price the sales committee said. One or two people showed interest in it, and they were asked this price. To make it a store, they said a renovation was too much. Also, the taxes are about one thousand dollars per week, because the town fathers are hardly Catholic. This was a put-off too. After the improvements, the building was appraised at nearly two million to set the taxes, but really the value in land alone is there."

"Tell her three hundred thousand dollars from a friendly patron and a quick closing in two weeks."

"Why, Rosario? Why waste money?"

"Julie, we are setting a course now. Publicity. We want top dollar from the customers. Gossip gets around. Let it be known we are not cheap ourselves. We have only just begun. I also want Grace to show it to me, so I can think about remodeling. Ten percent down on signing, and no mortgage back. If they are worried about funds, I will deposit the balance in forty-eight hours after signing with the title company. Okay?"

"Okay, Mr. Boss, but it rubs me over to pay. I get why, but money came hard to us in Minnesota. Too many kids to feed maybe. It still irks me to overpay for anything—shoes, milk, you name it."

"I understand, Julie, but let's do it my way this time. It will pay off. Use your talents to earn us top dollar when we open. Don't worry about the costs now. I am going to overspend a lot to get open faster and bring in my own men over from France, if need be, to supervise."

"It's your money, Rosario. To say the obvious, the more you, spend the better it is for my twenty percent, but it's me telling you not to do it. It's honest. You get it?"

"Julie, when you see the building inside again, think about where you want to stay rent-free so I can build out a suite for your liking. See which way you want to look out and on what floor. I would think the third, because the regular help will be on two, and you don't have to stay there just to save me money. When I leave someday, you will take my space on four, if you like. It's up to you, but don't go cheap on me to save me a few thousand dollars. It's not our deal, and it's not what I want. My space will be with no cost spared, and yours should be too. No discussion, and thank you for a job well done. Now do you want to eat or not?"

"I think I did a good job, too, Rosario. I'm too excited to eat and won't calm down for a while. I really wasn't sure if the whole deal was true. Now I want to get on with it: call Grace, go over the contract details, get her onto the liquor license, and try to sew it up. How do you want to own the building?"

"We need a corporation. We need a lawyer. Ask her for the names of people in her congregation. I want to use at least one of them, and I want a Catholic. The best is to name a holding company by the street address. We will need a second one for the liquor license, and we need an insurance person for policies. She will know."

"I agree. Let's get on with it. There will be plenty of time to eat later, and I have a lot of thinking and planning to do."

"Off with you, Julie, and tell me anytime you need anything. Also, let me know what Grace says and how to reach you discretely."

She stood, smiled, resisted giving him a kiss on the cheek, and handed him a folded paper with her address and cell phone, together with Grace's card. She was still one step ahead of him, but he was happy about it.

CHAPTER SIXTEEN
A Done Deal

Mississippi people—even Catholics—didn't look a gift horse in the mouth. They took the three hundred dollars after waiting overnight for all the board members to agree. Closing was in two weeks or less. They gave over the back title and the original building plans from the church's vault from sixty years or more before the new construction.

Things were moving fast, the speed Rosario liked best. *Give me action every time,* he thought. Julie was also in high gear. She gave notice to the Holiday Inn that she was moving on. She gave her already scheduled shifts away and went to work full-time with Rosario. Together, they formed real estate and separate liquor license holding corporations, which she alone owned, borrowing the money from Rosario, who filed a lender's lien on it. They spent only twenty-eight thousand in buying and transferring the license, and there were no objections. This took only a couple of weeks from start to finish and was actually done a few days before the real estate closing. All of it was funded by Rosario's on-hand funds and another half million that he had wired in to help with the renovation.

With Rosario's emerging comrades onsite, men were studying the plans for the build-out. But Julie was involved in all of it, freely expressing her ideas and opinions without holding back. A group of equals was coming together in workmanship. The three comrades had been introduced to

Julie as French *amis* without more explanation. Rosario made no mention of the corps.

The legion and its men were all well-rounded in their development. If something in an encampment needed building, they didn't call in any corps of engineers. They built it themselves; some with more formal training than others, and some with more practical experience. At heart, they were all builders, architects, and engineers as well as home-taught carpenters.

Rosario's *amis* would not be doing the building themselves but supervising it. Rosario wasn't out to save money, and he certainly didn't want to waste time getting it finished much later with only a few men rather than sooner. Hiring a large gang of men to literally bang it out would also announce his local presence, spread his money around, and get a mystique about him going around Jackson. It would cost a lot more, but it got the game going.

He advertised for qualified workmen in various skill areas—plumbers, electricians, carpenters, sheet rockers, masons, painters, and the like. He would not use a local general contractor, because he needed no oversight. When he had his crew together, he sought approval from the building department, which was immediately forthcoming. He hired a well-ensconced architect who was Jackson born and bred; he was pricy but influential. Along with the local hired tradesmen to whom he had committed, the architect also supported the project. The permits and inspections by municipal oversight officials were all approved without revision.

He would spend an estimated $350,000 or more on workmen in the next month or so to do the build-out, which that was a real shot of outside money into the local economy for Jackson. His labor figure did not include purchases of materials from local stores or insurance, paving the lot, paint, and food for the men, which he provided while they were on the job, especially if they worked late or overtime.

He had set out to capture the local spirit in his favor and had done so. People had already begun talking well about Rosario and the project. It was getting some local news play too, all of which was favorable.

There was no doubt that the place was already known to be a showplace from top to bottom. The front was reworked in a wooden veneer with pillars from roof to ground, which gave the front the appearance in stark white with gold leaf of an antebellum slave owner's big house. It was a mansion facade worthy of Huey Long himself, even if he did come from the next state south. Huge muted flood lamps drowned the building in a hazy light, making it look like an approaching star the closer people drove to it.

All customers were to be greeted on arrival on a triple-wide, semicircular, covered driveway that extended forward off the building thirty feet in both directions from the midpoint to keep any sun or bad weather from the honor guests. All cars would be parked by valets, and however untraditional for Mississippi, there were more than enough young women to see to prompt service. Julie had found them at her university, and they had top pay for little energy.

Locals were favored in hiring to help with the image. Tipping was not allowed, and all such gestures were to be politely declined at the risk of dismissal from the job, which paid the local college students more than enough. Generous drinkers were taken home, and their cars were brought with them. This was an extra service, for which they could tip. Unknown to the customers and not really understood by the college kids, which included women (however untraditional for Mississippi), assiduous records were kept of who was taken home, when, and by whom. These would be reviewed every week by Rosario to see if there were any trends and to see who of note was a drunk or going to a female friend's home or the like. He was collecting dirt.

Records would also be kept of the drunken drivers' guests and how often they came and had to be taken home as well as their attitude with the staff (either too friendly or nasty). Table arguments were to be noted by servers and likewise points of discussion. Casual or infrequent guests were not to be so written up, nor were travelers who had been told not to miss a trip to the "Mansion"—as what had started as "Rosario's Place" had come to be renamed by the locals. The help was not to talk about these private details to anyone. Most got free room and board and were paid very well. All were hired only by Julie, who screened them if they were not her friends from before, which most were. Each had secure employment by contract and, in return, had a trade secrets nondisclosure agreement with penalties for violation, starting with termination. To mask inquiry of any overriding purpose for such information, additional facts were also to be innocently gathered, including birthdays, favorite foods, drinks, wines, children, and pet names, nature of employment, and any other items that seemed to be tidbits to the servers.

After opening, a form was provided to servers for completion by the following day of the nightly service with the biggest area being for special observation comments. Each report generated five dollars or one hundred dollars for the server, if she had the best report of the week as rated for most detail and content. The competition to write the best report was soon properly understood well by the staff. The car service employees had no form, but they could submit an incident report if they wished. The best reasons to do so were if a patron became ill from too much drink or if any domestic discord occurred during the ride to the patron's destination. These were required for insurance reasons and similarly compensated. The casual help drivers did not know what the servers were obligated to report. There were no fill-in casual servers, and all groups—kitchen help, cleaners, maids, and special events workers—were kept separate without crossover to different jobs.

The money flowed from both ends and was controlled in the middle by Rosario. Good help made top dollar, and the patrons paid top dollar. The minimum price per head could easily be one hundred dollars, just like at a wedding. If patrons wanted a special meal (any dish of their liking), they could call it in with the reservation and add twenty dollars for each such entrée. If the patrons canceled, they still paid the meal add-on. Few did, and this allowed the staff to be fairly certain who would be coming in on a given evening and locate patrons where they wanted to sit, including if the party wanted one of a half-dozen private dining rooms of various sizes reserved in order to avoid the main floor crowd. All such parties could choose their servers, if they wished. Nightly regulars—of which there were more than a few, a good core of thirty to forty guests—needed no reservations unless they wanted special dishes or private rooms.

Corned beef and cabbage, chicken paprika, beef stew, and other special foods formed an endless list and covered all ethnic backgrounds. The tables were not turned. There were no double sittings. Patrons came in at seven p.m. and stayed until closing at two a.m. if they wished. Regulars wandered in a little early. No one was served past two a.m. to keep strictly within Jackson's liquor ordinances. There were no power breakfasts or luncheon meals.

The only exception was death. If a regular customer had bereavement (a family loss), she needed only to call and set forth approximately how many people were coming and at what time. They were politely told that the event needed to be over by six p.m. to allow for setup, but they could start at any time they wanted, since with a funeral, it would not be over before noon at the earliest. Prices were not discussed, and the bill was mailed.

The business style evolved by trial and error over the first two months. The public did no boycott Rosario's place, rather they flocked to it. Rosario's spreading of the seed money had proved clever and had primed the pump of success to get everything moving first class. A mystique developed.

Julie was on the floor greeting guests and putting out early fires at the start, finally knitting her army of workers into producing well-orchestrated performances night after night. The malcontents every restaurant did not enjoy were weeded out, and their reservations were politely declined until they got the message. It was plain. Patrons had to work their way in, even at top dollar, and if they were troublemakers, they were history. Drinking was no problem. Patrons being mean to their own guests was their business. But if patrons were foul-mouthed or loudmouthed to the help ... beware! Philanderers were all accepted. If they used their hands, cursed, or argued with the staff from the car park to a toilet attendant (all black and uniformed, of course), and they were toast, out of there for good. Cheap was not a problem; many regulars wanted a thirty-dollar bottle of wine rather than a fifty-dollar one night after night, but if they argued about a bill or did not pay it, they were gone!

Rosario believed that somewhere in his developing list of favored guests were the people who had laid him low or helped. They wouldn't risk predictable banishment but rather hang in being drained lower and lower into his intellectual filter. Sooner or later, they would sparkle out to him and be revealed. It was a matter of time, and he didn't think it would take as long as his stay in Biloxi's prison had been. They would be revealed sooner and by their own hand, their own behavior or chitchat.

To move things along more quickly, Rosario provided various encouragements. He came down nightly between nine and nine thirty and stayed until midnight or longer, as he chose. For an hour or so every evening, he and Julie together visited all of the guests' tables, giving either a casual hello to the unknown or briefly pulling up chairs with the regulars so those patrons would not need to stand.

On arrival, all regular or established repeat guests were served light house refreshments in the huge barroom, if they chose, or at their table. What they drank was already computer profiled and prepared by the servers' prearrangements of their tables at six p.m. each night. It was a small matter, but it made the repeat guests feel important, recognized, and most welcome.

His own *amis* were not idle, and each was identified as a maître d'. They keenly observed all the guests, reporting their own internal reviews and comments. The three of them reviewed these twice a week with Rosario, looking for any suspicions or for important people, among them guests whose help or knowledge might be called upon as needed.

Nothing was left to chance. Nothing was unplanned or as seemingly innocent as it appeared, but no one seemed to pick up on it. Julie had to be aware that all was not as it seemed, but she did her job as promised, stayed out front, ran a most successful evening every night, except Sundays as a family day in Jackson when the Mansion too was closed. So it went six days a week, day in and day out.

CHAPTER SEVENTEEN

Filtering Down

At about the fourth-month mark in operation, Rosario was certain that his prey was in the center of regulars. "Keep your friends close and your enemies closer," he knew as the age-old proverb. The guilty would need to be near him, drawn like a moth to flame, observing him, trying to figure out what he was about and why he was still around, being so successful and of apparent good cheer. He knew that, to them, it would make no sense; he should have fled long ago, but there he was sticking to Jackson like flypaper.

Everyone envied his success, his Mansion, his Julie, and his business vision. Anyone could have done it, but he was the one—a foreigner no less and without local help. How could a convicted murderer be savvy enough to pull it off? Who was he, and why was he so competent? What was he really doing if not searching them out? Where did his money come from? Why wasn't he afraid of them and on the run, afraid to get jammed up again maybe for good this time?

These were the questions Rosario knew the guilty must be asking. It would lead to their own disclosure, because they needed to act to get the answers. Standing by wasn't going to do it. Nothing had come of it so far for them, so they would need to take action when it finally became too fretful just to go with the same old routine, seeing if they could shake him up, get rid of him and the continued threat of his presence and his subtle prying into them. It had to be getting more nerve-wracking for them the more popular the Mansion became locally, and Rosario with it.

The image of Rosario and Julie moving through the guests each evening calm and accommodating enhanced their local acclaim. Locals were referring to them as though they were Bogart and Bacall in Jackson's *Casablanca*. In daytime if they were about, people would stop and stare and point them out like movie stars to their friends or children, recounting their last visits to the Mansion. People left them alone just like actors who came to live in their community instead of another place. It was like Eastwood in Carmel; no one disturbed him. He talked to people or not, and that was the way it was. These local people (the innocents) wanted most of all to keep Rosario and Julie around and to share in their presence however vicariously. No one dwelt on his past, which gave him the new chance all were allowed by law and Christianity once they paid their dues. Rosario and Julie were so lionized. Neither opposed nor encouraged it; they were just themselves, which was more than enough for Jackson.

Frenchy started the ball rolling during the biweekly review session on the fourth floor. The three comrades stayed sometimes at the farm and sometimes on the fourth floor but always together. Julie knew they went somewhere, but she had never been to the farm or been told about it. She accepted that there were secrets. She had elected to stay apart, being both female and not French. She was not clear about what they were up to, although she had a pretty good idea. If trouble came, she wanted to be somewhat distant to avoid blame or being picked on. She thought they knew it, because they did not bring her into their circle by sharing even dirty little secrets they might have in the past.

She may have been a little schoolgirl when it started over a half year before, but she wasn't stupid. The three men were not casual friends. They had all been close, regardless of age, for a long time, but they were not related or even of the same background. They were all disciplined and paid great attention to their health and conditioning, each spending several hours a day in the third-floor gym, working out vigorously to keep more than toned. Age didn't matter. They were each in better condition than any of the staff or help.

Kroper, the oldest, had told her to live well, and for a long time he had been saying that she should take to the gym. He had said that, if she wanted, he would train her so she could learn how to do it for herself in later years. None of the other men had really approached her personally. He was older than her father, but age did not seem to matter among them. No one of them was more or less than the others' equal, even considering age, money, or smarts, because they were all both clever and book-learned.

The three were marked, but not Rosario. Each had an upside down tattoo of a small cross on the left arm between the elbow and the wrist. Unless their cuffs were rolled high, she could not see their markings, and the cross faced them, so it looked only like a strange mark that was no more than an inch long and not of regular tattoo ink but a very deep blue. Kroper's was the palest, so age must have something to do with it showing how long he had had it.

She had looked to find out more on the Internet one night late when they had all been gone, but she hadn't found it. She gave it up in part because Rosario didn't have one. She thought it didn't bind them all, so she should not dwell any longer on it.

She was both right and wrong. It was a sign known to legionnaires, a silent mark of identity. Someone had to know what it was and had to have paid his dues to earn one in the ranks. He didn't get it by signing up. He signed up for his own reasons—hiding, running, or whatever. He only got it when he re-enlisted, making the legion his home and the other men his family for life. Once re-enlisted for another six years, he would sign up again and again until he couldn't anymore, because he was dead, too torn up, or ready to die. His chances of retirement—with no more "one for all and all for one" or recall for special projects like Rosario's—were about as good as a Don leaving the mafia. He didn't do it standing up. What she didn't know was that Rosario was eligible for the tattoo. He would have had it long before if he hadn't been set up. It was really a rite of passage and hardly done on the fly. A party followed the ceremony. It was a legionnaire's bar mitzvah without the gifts.

Little did she know that, being peaceful in her innocence. Good for her. On Sunday, Julie thought that she would ask Kroper about it. He had brought her into the gym two months before for two hours a day. Now like them, she knew that she was as fit as she could ever be and enjoyed it. She had surpassed herself, and Kroper had told her she had surpassed them all, not because she had set out to best them but because of her attitude and vigor toward it. The other three had not encouraged her, leaving it to Kroper, but in no manner had they criticized her. They all worked out with her as schedules and routines permitted, and each treated her as an equal. They spotted her, and she spotted them. It worked well.

After it was clear that she was committed and not a quitter or a bellyacher about abject pain from conditioning, Kroper told her there was something much more important that she should learn. She had no clue, and gave him a course reply, because he had disturbed in her concentration in the middle of her workout.

"What?"

"To use your hands, Julie."

"For what, Kroper?"

"For yourself. To protect yourself against unwanted men or women. Self-defense."

"Where do I learn that, Kroper?"

"Right here, Julie. From me."

"You're on, Kroper, but not today."

"Take your time, Julie."

So it began. Julie delved into the martial arts, sparring with all the men. She learned what they each knew. She took hard falls and really hardened up, kind of becoming one of them, by choice this time. She no longer kept her distance.

She paid the price though. Worry came naturally to her. She became fearful of when it would all end and, except for money, she would be back where it all started again, alone and without true friends. They were coming too soon to their last days. It made her sad, but she resolved to enjoy her new life as much as she could for as long as it lasted, living in reality and not living in the fantasy of projected futures.

Frenchy had been busy in past weeks, cross-referencing the names and events in the computer's history, looking for identities and patterns as well as anomalies of unique events that might stick out. His focus had narrowed again to the regulars. He ruled out the out-of-town, infrequent, or casual guests, most of whom were vacationers or just too distant or unrelated to Jackson with no roots in the community. He knew who they were from the records kept. If patrons were not regulars, they were asked to sign in and were told, if any explanation was requested, that it was for insurance or security reasons. The log contained places for full address, phone number, and e-mail. The patrons' guests also signed in. If they declined but paid with credit card, the server would ask the card company for full information to check the guest's payment, which was recorded with a log note of the guest's refusal. The circumstance was usually the same: the guest was in the company of someone (usually a younger woman but sometimes a man) with whom he should not have been.

Cutting the list further, Frenchy ruled out the guests who were Black, Jewish, infirm, quite elderly, or students. He had a reason for each exclusion, knowing it wasn't perfect but probable. Jews were out because of the church location and the cross carvings. Blacks were out, because it was unlikely that they would be killing and carving up whites. So it went as he filtered down again and again, looking at what was left in the distant categories, his remainder groups getting smaller and smaller.

When they were all settled as customary, Frenchy was the first to speak other than greetings and some small ribbings. The others agreed and accepted his leading the overall examination as his field of study. He was the intelligence officer. No one else wanted the job—just the solution for Rosario's sake.

Sometimes at these work sessions in the months past, Frenchy asked to have some information verified or backtracked. These were detail areas the others could easily try to resolve not, so they wouldn't take up Frenchy's energy to do it, which left him free instead for the real analysis. Such research was mostly to confirm what Frenchy already saw as dead ends, but he needed to be more certain and did not want to filter someone out in error. Usually the story was the same in the end. A guest from far away

in or out of Mississippi had come in with someone more local. The guest
was out, but what about tablemates? They were all checked out as to prior
visits and family relationships (usually developed by cross-referencing the
servers' reports as to whether they were family; for example, an uncle
taking a local niece to dinner).

It usually proved to be that sort of exclusion, but all members of the
party had to be reviewed before any were ruled out. It was a matter of
thoroughness. Frenchy had thought of assigning a probability of exclusion
rating to these people (weak, medium, or strong), but he had decided against
it. The issues were already too cloudy to be certain of which category level
was proper for any later review. He thought it unreliable. If he had to recheck
those who were filtered out again if they came up dry, he would check them
all equally and not based on some amorphous rating protocol.

The more Frenchy worked the lists, the more certain he became of
one feature, and so he spoke up, knowing it was time to commit to his
conclusion.

"*Mes amis,*" he said, setting a serious tone, "I believe we know where
to concentrate. All roads, in my mind, lead only to the forty or so regulars
and their families who come with them or their repeat guests. I think it
lies still more within the regulars themselves and not so much in those
who come with them, who I think are more of a mask, let's say part of the
disguise. Our presence here is such that I believe, in profiler terms, that
the prey are drawn to Rosario. They need to be close to him to watch him
and evaluate him and perhaps even test him with their discussions of values
or principles. I have little doubt about it. I have decided to put the others
aside and concentrate on the regulars now one by one, if need be, and no
longer in groups. Anyone disagree?"

No replies came, which was not abnormal or impolite. This was his
field of study, not theirs. If they wanted to kill someone by hand, they
asked Kroper. If they needed someone cut, they asked Rosario so it went.
If they needed to find a killer in a wood pile, they asked Frenchy. It was
no good treading on another man's specialty. They would reveal the killer
or killers, making them act out to spontaneously expose themselves by a
desperate act overloading by finally perhaps attacking Rosario.

"No," Frenchy said. He knew what he was about. It might not be perfect, but it was the best they had after the months of hard work.

Rosario broke the silence.

"Frenchy, you're the boss. We do it your way but not yet. We've been at it hard for a half year with the build-out details and opening. At holiday time, we put it aside for two weeks and then come back. Take R and R. Go home if you want. See America, but no working on the project. It's time for us to freshen up the mind. Doctor's orders."

The men agreed, but each knew no one was traveling. They would stay put, even if not on the investigation for a few days. The field reports would come in, and with a little extra work, they would all be logged in and screened. Nothing would be lost except a few days' time.

Frenchy spoke up, "If we are down to a particular group—the regulars—and we have looked at them already to filter them down, are we going to revise the focus of examination?

Rosario, we need to look at them another way, but I am not sure how," Frenchy continued. "We need new glasses for sure, but what is the prescription?"

Rosario filled it.

"How do you feel about Julie? Time for her to enlist and join the ranks?"

Everyone knew that Kroper knew her best. He had set her to training and taught her hand to hand combat, taking her under his wing.

"To what degree, *mon ami*?" he asked. "The legionnaires take no women in the ranks. Good reasons not to. Why now, and what about when payback time comes around? Are we going to leave her out then or dirty her up, not knowing how she will live with it? For us, there is no problem, but for her, who knows?"

Rosario would not decide, but he could speak to it.

"She knows what we are about even if she does not understand that payback has no limits. She knows she is still on the outside looking in. It's not a loyalty test. She has good instincts, and we may be stuck. We need to try better with the regulars and maybe change, or let's say enhance, our investigation to get information. She may have better thoughts on how to do it than we do. She may look at it differently, come up with the solution. Thereafter, we do our best to keep her out of the final solution," he said, using a term they all understood. "Think about it. We all have a veto. Anyone says no, it's done and over."

Waiting was unnecessary. These men deliberated quickly. It had kept them alive over the years of campaigns and early deaths for others. No one needed to sleep on it. Speaking up they all agreed to bring her in. It was a matter of how. Who should speak to her and should it be—altogether or one by one or just Kroper or Rosario? The decision was to have just Rosario talk to her. He had found her, brought her in, and made the deal with her. It had begun with him and her, and they agreed it should go forward (or not) in that way. If she consulted with one of them about it, that would be her business.

The meeting was over, and they all went their separate ways to think about it some more. While they had all agreed with no vetoes, it troubled each of them. But no one spoke up, instead keeping their reservations to themselves. The goal—payback—was one thing, but at what price? For themselves, no price was too high, but no one wanted her to pay any price at all. She should suffer no consequences, and that, they all knew, was a fantasy at best. There was always a price to pay, even if it was in their own minds. Time would tell, even if they didn't want to look it in the face to realistically consider what it could cost Julie.

CHAPTER EIGHTEEN
No Real Choice

Men can be so silly, Julie mused. *Too much testosterone. They never see the whole picture or look at things from my point of view, just plain male blindness. It is not ego but a lack of cleverness that seems innate to women. Probably that is why "the weaker sex" live longer and, if truth be told, end up controlling the vast amount of the world's wealth. Look at the Queen Mom, Leona Helmsley; niceness is not a necessary playing card. Longevity is.*

Sunday came, and the morning workout they usually all made it to was winding down. There was only a duty-free day ahead. They were all now cayenne hot and sweating, each drinking his choice of bottled fluids with or without electrolytes. Julie loved those mornings, which pumped her up for the rest of the day's energy. She knew she was among friends.

Rosario finished happy and started heading to shower upstairs. On the way out, he passed Julie and asked if she was free to join him for a while to talk. It had occurred many times before. She was used to it. The other men picked upon it, but they did not see it so innocently. They knew what was coming. She was not exactly a lamb led to slaughter; she still had her own free will or so they thought.

"See you then in half an hour, okay? I'll be upstairs working. Come whenever."

"Half an hour, Rosario. How long do we need? I have plans to see some friends from college. A baby shower at two this afternoon."

"Probably ten to fifteen minutes I think. Certainly not much more than that. You'll have plenty of spare time to meet up, or we can do it later or tomorrow if you want."

"No business first. See you later," she said, returning to finish her last cycle on the treadmill. He left.

She left the elevator on the fourth floor and joined Rosario while still in her workout clothes with a large towel around her neck and shoulders. She was cooling down. It was still early but the sun was streaming in the windows. He sat with his back to them, getting warm. He saw her glowing in the sunlight and was reminded of how attractive, how vibrant and alive she was. Her skin was perfect, and she looked elegant, even in moderate disarray after her workout. That was a thought he seldom had. He wondered why he had it now, but he put it aside. *Business first*, he agreed with her in his head.

"Julie, you know we are looking into my problem. We discussed this at first, before the Mansion got started. You have helped my friends, who are here to guide me. We think the people we are looking for are already known to us among the regulars, but we are stuck. Maybe we have tunnel vision and are not looking at it properly. It happens when you are too close to the topic. We need a fresh point of view—yours, if you are willing. We need some way to sort it out—a woman's point of view, let's say."

"Okay" she replied, still not sure what it all meant but not at all surprised that she was finally being asked to really join in.

"It's complex. We don't understand where we have painted ourselves, maybe, into a corner and how to get us out. You need to consider the techniques we used to help us out. Frenchy can fill you in. Tell you what he ruled in or out, so you can look at it from your point of view."

"Okay," she said again and nothing more. She did not ask what the end result would be when they had the answer.

"It's up to you, Julie. You don't have to pitch in. There's no battle pay. It's really completely voluntary. In or out changes nothing. We go on as before."

"In," she said. "In for a penny, in for a pound." She could have told him she was happy to be finally accepted and asked to join, but she didn't still being unsure that he would properly understand. Rosario wasn't not clever, quite the contrary. Instead, he seemed naïve, including about her and women. It had to be his upbringing, whatever that had been, she had concluded in earlier days. Her thoughts about him guided her view to leave her personal conclusions alone and just agree to help.

She wasn't mooning over him, though he was rich, obviously smart, and attractive, even if somewhat humorless with her. More bothersome, he remained obtuse, giving her no come-on or any encouragement in their own relationship. He could be so charming with the guests, but that was all self-motivated. When it came to her, he seemed not to be self-starting.

Maybe she was to blame. They had a business deal. It was clear from the get-go. She had done little or nothing except his bidding to warm him up, to get him going. Maybe she was the cold fish. Maybe he was actually shy. Maybe she had put too much stock in winning him over just by doing her job well, looking for endorsements that would never come just because she had kept her bargain. Maybe he was already married, betrothed, or spoken for. *Maybe he is gay*, she thought for the first time, *but what a waste if so.* Maybe he had been traumatized. Maybe she would never know. Maybe it would be best to give it up now and earn her keep while looking elsewhere for comfort. Time would tell. This would be especially true sooner, now that she was moving within the inner circle.

Nevertheless, she finally decided that Rosario was, at best, not clever with her. It was his reluctance and not hers. She could not believe he was inexperienced with women, but with what kind? He was no gold digger. A lot of women guests—some of whom were really wealthy and the others who were married (or not) but libertines—had set their eyes on him. Many had tried to fall into his waiting arms, but she had seen it was useless for them. He wasn't interested and not taking that road to even just pass time without commitment.

Even some of her friends with youth on their sides had spoken up about his being everything and asked why she hadn't gotten her nails into him yet. He was a catch all right, but what would she be catching? Maybe being on the inside, she would find out.

She thought about it more and more as the day passed. She was aloof at her party that afternoon as she became more preoccupied with his offer itself. It was not because she was unwilling to be of help but because of how revealing of him it seemed. He had no insight into her, into them. How did he think paying and overpaying a barely employed hotel hostess, making her part of a business and exposing her to luxury overnight would not affect her?

There was the real befriending of the other men, his *amis*. Those guys were at least as charming in their own rights, and to all observers, she was part of their team. The local mystique had fallen on her, too, because of these associations. It was all like a Hollywood movie, and she was left wondering when the pinch on the cheek would wake her up and it would all be over.

They were all so far out already and bonded, how could he even think to ask if she was in or out? What choice did she really have? If she said no, she risked waking up and losing it all. The more she thought about it, the more it made her mad. It wasn't that Rosario was a dope or mean-spirited, but he wasn't thinking realistically in human terms. He was not relating to her or thinking about it from her point of view at all. He wasn't taking her for granted. He just wasn't thinking about them and about her, and that was a problem, a big problem. Sure, she knew that they all had some program of payback and wanted her out of harm's way. She knew that. What else was new? If he was offering her in, was there going to be a change in their relationship? Would it be better or worse? She thought better if he had to rely upon her more. What if she brought him the gold ring? Would she get one herself as her reward for getting to the bottom of it all? It was all becoming too much to think about.

She finally put her thoughts aside, getting back into her party and friends with a chuckle on one last thought. Maybe she should have Kroper train her up hard for the next few weeks and then kick Rosario's ass when they hit the gym next time.

Let's see what he thinks about that and little miss girly!

CHAPTER NINETEEN

Who's on First?

When the party was over and she was back at the Mansion, Julie let no moss grow cold under her. She rooted out Frenchy, who was downstairs cooking himself a meal in the full kitchen. When their greetings were done, she asked him to give her the list of the regulars and all of the reports on them by cross-reference. He smiled and told her it would take him until the next day, because while the list was easy, the cross-references from the reports would take some time to coordinate a full list for each one.

She asked him separately to tell her if any of the regulars were on the same reports or in other words, buddied up with each other. He agreed and silently noted to himself that he liked her get-up-and-go attitude. She was not wasting time but rather getting right into it—all business when she had to be, even if a lot of fun when off duty.

He wondered where Rosario's mind had been. How he could not have set his eyes on her instead of keeping only to business Frenchy didn't grasp. He had partied with Rosario and knew that he like women, but where was he now? Missing in action? Maybe he was biding his time, waiting to see what happened when they were all done and if he was still standing on both feet. It was not his business really, but he still thought it was odd. Rosario was a guy who had come stateside looking to settle down. Here was warm apple pie right in front of his nose, and now he wasn't hungry anymore. It was strange.

Frenchy began to tell Julie how he had whittled down to the regulars and what he had concluded so far. She stopped him at once, telling him she wanted her own clear view of it. She didn't want her mind prejudiced going in. She said they could talk about it after she felt done with her own analysis. She was unsure of how long it would take or what she would find.

Boy, he liked that young girl! She made her own way, with no doubt about her own abilities. She was full of self-confidence, and that was well deserved. She knew her own strength and abilities.

Rosario was really missing the boat. It was too bad. This find alone could have made all of his troubles worthwhile. Frenchy thought that many a lad would give up a year or two to find the right match, a lifelong bargain that was worth the while. He was beginning to question if Rosario was really as clever as everyone thought. He could quit now and just stand aside and let only the good times roll rather than let them pass him by because he was stuck on some concept of vengeance.

All of it was turning out not to be such a smart idea. It was the old joke: "I went to a fight, and a hockey game broke out." Rosario had come looking for love. He had found hate and evil, and but then he had a real chance at family and couldn't see it, because he was blindly stuck on revenge. Maybe they were all keeping him from wising up. They were perking him up artificially. If they quit him, maybe he could leave it alone and find his own way back to a normal life with Julie or at least a more nominal one.

Maybe Frenchy would chat with the others about it and see what they thought, but not yet. He wanted to wait it out a little longer and learn what Julie came up with, what he missed. There was no harm there. Nothing seemed to be heating up, so he could wait it out.

CHAPTER TWENTY
Surprise

Julie had had the guest list for over a week without saying anything. Time wasn't wasting because the boys were still on holiday, even if she was hard at work with her regular duties as well.

On Wednesday morning early—too early for her now that she was into a routine ending at two a.m. and not asleep until at least three a.m. A nine thirty call was disturbing to her routine. The cell phone never rang that early, and very few people had the number. The boys were onsite, so they would not have called if they needed her. She answered, not knowing who it could be.

"It's me, Julie," was the greeting.

It made no sense to her. She couldn't connect the voice to a name.

"Who?"

"Julie, it's me, Grace Trouller, your broker. I found the mansion for you." She no longer called it the YMCA.

She had come in once or twice early on after it opened but not since. It was a lot of money for her to pay with a guest or two, and Julie had seen that she was comped. Maybe the price kept her out, but many people (casual guests but no regulars) had come in saying that she had sent them along. So what could it be months later, Julie wondered.

"Julie, I know it's unusual and that you're not selling the Mansion, but yesterday I had a call asking about your place. He wanted to know what it cost you and if I would see if it was for sale. I was surprised, because the caller was a well-known old Mississippi lawyer from town whose father was governor long ago. He knows how to check the deed and the build-out costs at the tax assessor's office to find out. These records are public.

"I told him all I could do was find out and ask if Rosario is interested. He said he would pay my commission and to tell you so when coming to a price. I said thank you and hung up and found your number in my file. I didn't want to wait, both to not lose the deal if there is one and to let you know at once."

"Grace, I only have a small interest, but I can ask Rosario when he is around," Julie said, buying them time. She knew the price would be steep, if there was one at all. "I'll take it up with him when I can and let you know, but it will take a while. I'll call you in a few days or next week. Thank you for your help. Who is the buyer?"

"He didn't say Julie, and I didn't ask. It's not polite with lawyers. It's why they call and not the client. If he wanted to say, he would have. Have a good day!"

"Goodbye, Grace," Julie said, and then they were finished.

There were no house phones—all the lines were on the same system—and no intercom. That had been intentional to force them all to speak in person. Using her cell phone to call Rosario, even if he picked up, didn't seem to follow the rules. So up she rose, putting on her sneakers, jeans, and a college sweatshirt. Then out the door and up the elevator she went, calling to him when the elevator door opened.

"Hi, there," he said. He was already awake and having coffee with Kroper in the kitchen. He often left before she closed, and she did not know when that had been the night before. She knew they were all early risers who got up well before her, but they never brought it up. *A young girl needs her beauty sleep*, she thought as Frenchy and Louis filtered in, giving her their stout, warm hellos.

"I had a call just now from Grace Trouller, the broker," Julie said. "She had a call earlier from a lawyer with an undisclosed client wanting to buy the Mansion. She wanted to know if you would sell and obviously how much."

"Well, well, well," Louis piped up. "Finally they come alive, and someone wants us gone. *Why* we can guess. Who could it be? Looks like the pressure is beginning to work, Rosario. The tide is turning, and it's against your sticking around. Congratulations."

"We all agree?" Rosario asked.

Julie made no response. It was too soon for her, and she didn't think "we" yet included her. Kroper gave a "Maybe" back, and Frenchy just grunted "*Merde*" in his best nasal French, just like when he was heavy-lifting in the gym. No translation was needed. It came out not like a curse but more like appreciation for the time spent finally getting somewhere. It was a grunt of appreciation.

"We think about it until the next work session. Julie will be joining us so we can all speak our views, if need be. It's tabled until tomorrow afternoon at two, unless there are any questions."

"One. Who's the lawyer?" asked Frenchy. "Maybe I can back up his representational clients listed as references in the law firm's profile to some of the guests."

"Grace didn't say, Frenchy, but she was told his father had been governor. I'm sure that narrows it down for you. How many of those could there be? Two or three at best with lawyer sons of note in Jackson, if that?"

"Thank you, Julie. Well done. Thanks for not making us wait to hear it. Call Grace back and tell her you raised it with me already and I am thinking about it. Keep her people hooked. Maybe it's better to do it in person. Look her in the face and see what you think.

"I don't understand the game of cat and mouse about who the lawyer is. The client could stay hidden and still do a deal, but the lawyer would have to show up sooner or later or get a replacement. If he was going to do that, he would have already. Tell her when you're together that it doesn't make sense to me. Let's save Frenchy some research time. We should try to make sure that we've got the right man from the start, if it's multiple choice on a governor's son.

"Let me know when a meeting is set up. If you can, ask her in tonight for dinner. Tell her it's short notice and we are all busy but that, to move it forward, you would like to speak to her. Maybe I will join in briefly. Tell her you can't say for sure. Let's see what she does. I don't think it's her call."

CHAPTER TWENTY-ONE
Playing Cat and Mouse

Julie was sure that Grace was expecting a call back, but instinct told her it would be too quick if she did so when she got back to her room. She felt it would be too revealing and would almost confirm what they had been up to for the past many months. If it were up to her, she would have waited a day or two. On the other hand, maybe the businessman in Rosario would want to turn a good profit and move on to the next deal. The situation had many facets, she thought. She knew that payback was still the biggest.

At about four p.m. she called Grace back and extended Rosario's invitation as though it was her own. Julie tried to sound worried and pretended to give answers and instructions to staff for the evening while speaking to her. Grace said that she would call right back. Julie told her that she did not usually make reservations and told Grace what to say to Stephanie, knowing that she herself would not take the call. She told Stephanie just to book them in if Grace called and to note for her the time the call came in. Stephanie had the phones all day long, from noon on, for tables, food, and special orders. Without more details, she was simply to say that Julie was busy and had put her on the job. She was to ask when Grace would be coming in and how many would be in her party as well as whether there were any special food or other requests. She was to keep it simple and seem normal.

Not even five minutes later, Grace called back and was helped by Stephanie, but she was obviously miffed that Julie was too busy for her and unreachable. Southern women are not good with covering up their feelings of anger with each other. She wasn't unpleasant in spoken word but more curt and dismissive when Stephanie made it plain that her reservation would proceed through her. Stephanie was polite throughout, asking Grace again for special requests, knowing there would be two people about seven thirty. There was a request, but not for food or drink. Grace asked Stephanie to "Please ask Mr. Rosario to stop by during the evening, however briefly." That gave up the reason she so wanted to speak to Julie, whom she knew could produce the elusive Mr. Rosario.

"Does your guest have a name for the reservation book?" Stephanie asked. It came out naturally, because she always tried to get as much information as she could in advance. There was nothing unusual there. Grace said that it was just two in her name and left the gender of her guest out. *But in a way,* Julie thought when Stephanie had hung up—she had been eavesdropping on another muted line—*Grace has revealed their position by calling back so quickly.* They should have waited a bit like she had. It would have been better not to be so eager and to even wait a day or two. Obviously, whoever was pulling the strings was no longer patient enough to play the game.

Julie reported it at once to Rosario, who was still upstairs. He called Frenchy in with but a whistle. She wondered if they each had a special call. Maybe it was a French thing. She didn't want one—not now, not ever. At home, they had whistled only for the dogs, and that had been enough for her. She never had. She had called them by name, and they had always come.

Frenchy popped in at once, and Rosario filled him in, looking at Julie to make sure he said it all correctly.

Frenchy, himself unsure, asked, "Is that all of it?"

"Yes," Julie said.

Rosario wasn't finished and was trying to think a step ahead. "The governors' sons in the law business here can't be so large a crowd. Run it down, Frenchy, as soon as possible. I bet she is coming with Mr. Wonderful,

Esq., and I would like to be up on him. We need to let them know up front that we do our homework. Let me know as soon as you get it down. Julie, please stick around. I don't think it will take Frenchy all that long."

"On it, Doc," Frenchy said. He was already nearly out the door.

Frenchy was back in a quarter of an hour, all smiles. Rosario gave Frenchy a downturned lip despite his joy. So far, no one had used his comrade name, and it had just come out in the course of things. It was what they all called him, especially when upstairs at home. Julie hadn't missed it, but she didn't react either. *Who knew what,* she thought. Done was done. They didn't admonish each other. They were all in it together, helping him. It was a mistake but not a real one. She was on their side. Let her sort it out with him, if she cared.

"One is too old. Not active anymore but still listed as being 'of counsel' to the firm his father started. He is well into his eighties. The second one, Mr. Ross Gillmore II, Esq., is fifty-five or thereabouts. He has been in four times about a month apart and started the first week. I am printing out his servers' reports for you. He was never taken home. His father's dead two years ago, and his last term as governor ended nine years ago. It's is all I know for now, but I am running his firm down. Later, I will be cross-checking his guests and reading his reports. I'll pick up his table's photos for those nights too."

All guests arriving through the main entrance on the mansion's red carpet between six thirty p.m. and eight p.m. were greeting by Stephanie and videotaped. So far they had not delved into the tapes. Now they might be useful. He would see. For now, that was enough, and back Frenchy went to his computers and videos.

Off Julie went but with a smile all over her face. *Live and learn,* she thought.

"See you later, Doc," she said as the elevator door closed. It was the girl still in her. She couldn't resist. It was one more stepping stone of discovery, whatever the hell it meant.

He laughed at it too but she never heard it. It would have made her happy.

CHAPTER TWENTY-TWO
Getting Ready

Things were beginning to move very quickly. Everyone was trying to do their tasks both with extreme diligence and at top speed. No one was really in control, but everything was filtered through all of them. Rosario set the pace and set it hard. If anyone could be said to be in charge, it was Rosario, but he was really only a clearing center for information and coordination.

Louis had been sent out to the farm to bring it up to speed for any forthcoming private, unfriendly interrogation. After all, he was also the small arms man, and it looked like things might be moving in that direction. It was better to prepare than not to.

Louis had already started taking apart, cleaning, and test firing the former owner's hidden treasure trove of weapons. All of them, except two twelve-gauge Winchester bird guns, were World War II vintage military weapons. Louis knew what that meant. The guns were not registered, except maybe the shot guns. There were hundreds of thousands of handguns all over the world from the great wars. They were still fine machines and much better than more modern handguns. Advances had been made in long guns but not in the small arms pistols and automatics of yesteryear. A 1911 model of a Colt .45 was still the same as when the Colt .45 was patented. Except for add-on lasers or scopes, there was nothing to do to improve them.

Happily, Louis noted that almost the entire small arms collection was single rounded at 9 millimeters, which was a mighty fine shell. All of the handguns were sought after, because they were preregistration and could not be traced back to any owner by ballistics, unless someone had registered them. No one savvy about guns would be so foolish. Unregistered, the guns could bring five times or more of their registered value, even to collectors rather than users. The wall safe easily contained well over one hundred thousand dollars in such weapons, and Louis had made it clear that, at the end, he would be leaving with them for use or sale in the legion.

The one smaller weapon was an eight-shot beretta (a short nine) .380-caliber World War II Italian officer's gun with a well-worn back pocket holster, complete with the sheepskin-lined ankle strap for full concealment. Louis carried it when at the farm and kept it well hidden in a floor knockout in his room at the Mansion—"You never know when you'll need one" had been his lifelong motto. He had also put his arms supplier up north on hold, telling him to keep the five thousand–dollar deposit for a later rainy-day order if one ever came.

Louis had heard that Mormons kept six months' worth of food on hand as a tenant of their religion. Louis was no Mormon, but he knew the value of being well stocked. He was fully prepared with food, drink, and medicines of every type with batteries, bullets, and gasoline for at least a half-year siege—all of it bought over the months at sales at various stores to be less conspicuous. None of it had been delivered, and he had done the hard work of picking it all up and carrying it in. If there was some supply he had missed other than Ty-D-Bowl, he didn't know what it was, even though he kept going over it in his mind, trying to catch himself up. Flypaper? Dental floss? Who knows what? Sometimes people had to rough it. They would have to go with toothpicks. Those they had. If nothing else, Louis was thorough in the details (which was his job), and although it may not have been as online for tracking down Rosario's villain, he knew it was as important if they were all going to make it out in one piece when it was all over. It was like covering the back door, and he was good at it. It gave him pride.

While Louis was being the outfitter, Julie was still trying to develop a new strategy for opening up the regulars to draw whatever they knew or guessed out of them without them realizing it and making it appear to be a voluntary act. Pulling teeth was not happening. They needed to be induced to gossip or squeal, but she wondered how to drag it out of them in a restaurant environment. *How, how, how?* ran through her mind along with little more of substance. The daily setup and routines she delegated to Stephanie and some of the other staff in order to lighten the load and give her the freedom to think it all out. So far, she had been shooting blanks. She had had no luck at all.

Rosario was cool headed. He knew they were getting somewhere and exactly how he wanted to play it later on with their friendly broker. He was sure her guest would be none other than the well-known Ross Gillmore II, Esq., the governor's son. Since Gillmore had already been in four times, the records had to show what he called for a first drink. The custom of a returning guest being greeted with the poison of his choice was well known to the clientele. Handing him one on arrival would telegraph that he had already been exposed. This would put him on the defensive a little and loosen him up perhaps. It was innocent and a definite chess move in their favor.

Rosario called Stephanie himself, bypassing Julie because he did not want to bother her with such a small drink detail. Stephanie got back to him that she had checked the earlier visits and knew that he opened with a whiskey sour and that she would note that in the server's book. The broker was a white wine girl all the way, drinking Chardonnay, and she would be greeted similarly. It was a small detail, but it was now resolved.

He would let them sit and relax and order their food; they would be in the middle of their meal when he came down around eight thirty or nine p.m. That would give him some slight advantage. While they ate, they would talk creating disruption if not chaos. *Let them be put more off center*, he thought. Julie had comped their meal, in any event, so they could doggie bag what they didn't finish without regret. He doubted they would bother.

Rosario had also been thinking about his image. It was time to mix it up a little. Everyone knew about his place by now, but a little showmanship made sense. It was time for him to take it all to another level, especially if Julie came up with a solution to break the ice in the flow of the real information they actually wanted. It didn't take him much effort to come up with something.

The boys were all parachute-trained and jumpers from the airborne. Unlike large armies, the legion usually jumped six to ten men at a time in small assault companies as commandos who specialized in guerilla cut-and-run ambush techniques within enemy strongholds. There were no big C-47s for them. They jumped from helicopters big and small. Choppers pulled them out when needed and took home their dead and wounded. They ferried in the battle surgeons and nurses. In a real campaign, it looked like Vietnam under the Americans in *Apocalypse Now,* which had become a favored film among the legionnaires, even without any French in the cast. For a starter, cinematographer Caleb Deschanel had sure deserved his Oscar, Rosario believed. Now he wanted his.

Mississippi had very few helicopters. Rosario had been there long enough to know that was certain. He did not constantly see them overhead like in the larger American cities. Even the local news stations were truck mobile, and no traffic reporters used helicopters. There was no real road congestion. The governor had a mini one, and so did the state police, but he didn't see medevacs overhead constantly flooding into the hospitals either. He already knew that the Mansion's roof would hold a pad and, because of the solid 1950s construction, a large heavy chopper too. He was thinking of getting one. It would set him apart and enhance his mystique further. It would also be invaluable if they all had to cut and run; he could be in Cuba in two hours at high speed. Many of the older legionnaires were retired there, living the good life, even if still on recall. Leaving would be no problem, and in hostile battle, they had often changed the rondells in a few minutes' time, slapping on predesigned numbers and letters over the true legionnaire designations. He just didn't know if they were close enough to need to develop a full exit plan. Safe was better than sorry. He would bring it up when they were all together.

Frenchy was as busy as busy could be and getting absolutely nowhere in checking and cross-referencing the regulars and other guests for matching areas. The hits were too numerous to make any organized sense. The fields of focus were too broad, and he had to narrow them somehow. The areas that did match made no sense, and most similar entries numbered in the tens and twenties at least. It would take a whole police department to narrow them down by doing field work into the neverending future. It was a problem of too much information and little else. He needed a better route, but it wasn't coming to him. For now, he had to admit that he was stuck as he continued to trickle his search entries into his computer, looking for a reasonable result to evaluate and look into further. He had no such luck.

The only one still on holiday break was Kroper. He was still in the gym, even if he was lonely with no other company. His expertise had not been exhausted. It just had not been used yet. There were no candidates to interrogate, torture, or slaughter. He was sure there would be soon enough, but just not yet. He might as well keep getting ready by building his strength up, even if he didn't need to.

He was ready to go to work, indeed, as ready as he could possibly be and even anxious. He was a man who enjoyed a good workout. He appreciated a strong interrogation at the beginning. It gave him more to do and kept him busy, but it always had the same problem. It was nothing unique to him. It was known to all interrogators who plied their skills. The harder you worked at it, the more willing the subject became to tell you anything you wanted to hear to stop the torment. To get true results would take longer and, even, some periods of reserve and kindness—a drink, shower, a meal or two. It slowed the process down and still left him questioning, actually doubting, the information he was getting. He always tried to tell his subjects to avoid it and give it all up at the beginning. No one really listened, thinking they could best him. *Too much television,* he thought. *Fools.* If they could only listen to reason, they could save themselves the damage, even if the game had to be up for them in the end. *Quicker was better than longer, but just try to tell them with their deaf ears,* he thought. It was a good thing for him. He enjoyed his work.

He smiled to himself. He added another twenty pounds to the 150 he had already been bench-pressing. *Not bad. Not bad at all for an old man,* he thought. *Yes, I better strengthen up* was his last thought as he started the first of his thirty presses, knowing he had still a lot more weight to add before the workout was over. Everyone else was busy. There was no reason he shouldn't be. He would just have to bide his time, getting stronger and stronger.

CHAPTER TWENTY-THREE
Exposure

The six thirty p.m. regulars were coming in already, and soon enough, the doors would open for the reservation crowd. The cameras were on, and the tapes were running. The servers had decorated their tables carefully and checked the opening drinks for return customers as well as special requests and guest lists for known guests. Another night was beginning, and the money would soon be flowing.

One-meal-a-day service was not hard duty, and it was over in eight hours or less usually, as few guests stayed until closing. The longer they stayed, the more you made. Three to four hundred a night was quite usual, unless the customers were into fine wines, in which case, it could be more. Tips were added at a straight 20 percent, and the house took none of them. It was better money than the servers could earn anywhere else in Jackson, even if they did have to declare it and their taxes were taken out weekly. Free room and board made up the difference, and the servers were a loyal and happy lot. They knew on which side of life their bread was buttered.

At 7:25, Grace and her guest pulled into the horseshoe and up to the front entrance in the near right lane. Their doors were opened at once by valets. The driver was asked the name for the ticket, and Grace gave hers. The head valet used his wireless headset to call in the name to Stephanie, his voice coming through the miniature speaker on her desk. She put the arrival time down and got ready to greet them after a runner was sent to tell their server that they were in the house. No casino car park had a more competent system in spotting high rollers as they came in. At the Mansion, all guests were "whales," and the bills they paid for food and service proved it. At least in a casino, guests had a chance to leave without getting their pockets picked. At the Mansion, it was a one-way street in the Mansion's favor only.

Stephanie was both lively and highly verbal. She could tell proper and foul jokes with the best of them. She suffered as a Mississippi woman, because she was innately smarter than most of the other men and women she met, and it set her apart but not in her favor socially. Men were afraid of her, despite her balanced and virtuous appearance, which drew them toward her initially. Women were cleverer. They didn't want her around their men. It was too much of a challenge. Mississippi country club rules applied: Once a couple was divorced, only a man could stay on as a member. No one wanted an available woman around her man.

Stephanie greeted Grace and shook hands with her male companion. She introduced them to their server, Rosalind.

"Rosario asked me to tell you that dinner is on the Mansion tonight, and he will join you when he can. Enjoy yourself and bon appétit."

Stephanie smiled and stepped back to her podium, busying herself while they were led off to the economic slaughter that would pass them over that night.

Rosalind led them to the table and seated them, holding the seat for Grace. She nodded to her busboy, who came forward with a drink tray, and she placed a white wine and a bubble-glassed drink down before each of them.

"White chardonnay for the lady and a whiskey sour for the gentleman, if you please."

"Thank you," the broker said so politely in her Southern schoolgirl drawl.

"Thank you too, sweet," her companion said. "I'd prefer a Gibly's martini next, please. Thank you so much."

"Yes, sir, right away," Rosalind said, removing his drink and nodding to the busboy, who took it from her and hurried off to the bar. Inwardly, she was flustered, but she didn't show it. She had been one of the last servers to come on board, but she had been there for nearly two months. She had never been wrong on an opening drink, but of course she didn't supply the information. There was no protocol for such errors in their training. It was the unexpected, so she let it drop and continued with the menus.

She stepped back while the guests did their own homework. No male-only price list was included, because they were comp'd. Most men never bothered with it anyway. Only the wine list had prices, because it was state law for the sale of liquor. No one cared much about it either. They had a very rich clientele. A small card on each table announced that all mixed drinks were fifteen dollars except for liquors, with prices on request. No one ever asked. It wasn't polite in Mississippi. If someone was looking for a bargain on his night out at the Mansion, then he drank the bar choice and kept quiet.

Another server told Rosalind that she had an eight o'clock table coming in, so she excused herself. Stephanie spied her just before the new guests made it to her station.

"Everything okay on table six?" she asked Rosalind.

"Fine, Steph, but his drink was wrong. No big deal."

"Really?"

"Gin martini but no whiskey sour. Too sweet, he said."

Stephanie greeted her guests and turned them over to Rosalind. No more was said about the drink. Nevertheless, it bothered Stephanie. She had never been wrong before, and she had checked the drink herself. She was sure she hadn't gotten it wrong. She would check it again later, even if it was no big deal. Stephanie was plagued. She was an Aries, and staying perfect was important, however difficult it was in an imperfect world. She would check it again and not just once. If she had made the mistake, she needed to know. If not, how had it happen? "Too sweet" was not the reply of someone whose taste had changed. All gin—a neat martini—was a far cry from a whiskey sour.

She let it pass as she saw to incoming guests and made her table rounds inside the dining room, following up as she did each night.

Rosario usually came down early at eight forty-five p.m. When he entered the main dining room, the staff knew it and so did most of the guests who were still alert. He always approached Stephanie and Julie to say hello and to pick up on anything of note.

That night, he was dressed in an all-white Hong Kong–tailored linen suit over a pale blue Hermes shirt with cuffs and custom-made Chanel Chinese red loafers with a double C trademark metal band on the top. He looked comfortable, and the suit was casual, but it fit his frame well, even if it had been mail ordered and cut unfitted.

He had had it airmailed in only two weeks before and had his friend Goldstien fit and finish it. He gave the old man all of his business. Sometimes Goldstien came to the Mansion to fit him with swatches of fabric for him to pick from. Time and time again, Rosario had asked him to come to dinner and just bring his guests. The reply was always the same: "I'm just an old Jew who eats plain. What would I do here all night long?"

Rosario made sure that food for several nights was put in Goldstien's van whenever he left. He had the chefs try their hands at ethnic food, knowing that Goldstien couldn't find a good chicken-in-the-pot in Jackson. Maybe it wasn't gefilte fish, but there were plenty of soups (barley, chicken, pea) and briskets, corned beef, and health salads that Rosario could put aside for Goldstien. The first time, he did it not expecting anything in reply. The old man sent him a thank-you note, showing himself to be a person of manners. To Rosario's surprise, it contained an emblem of a hunting dog with crossed rifles at the top with the man's name imprinted below. He had left it out on his coffee table as a pleasant reminder of friendship.

Julie was on the floor working it alone, and he sidled up to her. They usually didn't speak. She knew the drill. If there was anything to say, she would let him know. If not, then she would just smile a silent hello, and he would pass on until they made the rounds together later. He would see the regulars himself and then do the reservations, usually with her putting forth the normal questions about food and service satisfaction. Julie would also ask the more personal guests questions researched from prior visits about sick relatives, business, or children and dogs—the whole nine yards. He would join in with either some prior remembrance or a typical observation. They worked every table; no guest was left behind.

Stephanie was at table six doing her own hello. He let her be, because he wasn't ready for that table yet. He thought he should let them see him greeting his guests in no real hurry to do business except on his own timetable. Stephanie cut loose and came over to him, figuring out that he wouldn't approach.

"All okay, Steph?" he asked.

"Amen, boss. All is well. One faux pas only and on your table six. The gentleman's drink call was wrong. I checked it myself this morning when you asked me to look into it. No whiskey sours but a neat gin. I'll check it later again. I don't like mistakes."

"No big deal, Steph. It's hard to stay perfect," he said with a big smile, almost a laugh. It was a joke of theirs. She was born on April 8, and he was born on April 6. They knew each other's story. He had got her because of their Aries sign for perfection. She gave out a real laugh and moved on.

It was time to go to work. He sidled up to Julie again. She was still making rounds. He waited for her to finish her table nine chitchat, not hurrying her along and even briefly joining the conversation. Then with his arm on her elbow, they approached their table six guests with the lounger already standing with his hand out. They shook.

It's nice to meet you, counselor. It's always nice to have the governor's family here. I am glad you could come. Good evening, Grace. You look charming and well. May I see to anything for you? Please sit down, Ross," Rosario said, using his first name as though they were established friends. "Enjoy your dinner, and we can talk later if you like."

"Now is fine, Rosario, unless you would prefer later."

Rosario made no answer but looked to the busboy. He said nothing but got across his message. He never looked unless he wanted something, and obviously now, it was chairs. Anything else and he would have told the server. When they were both seated, they were aware that Ross Gillmore II, Esq., knew that Rosario had done some homework in figuring out who he was. Gillmore knew it was time to move directly forward.

"What do you think about selling the Mansion, Rosario?"

"Well, it's not up to me alone. Julie is a part owner, and it's still new enough to be good fun. Making money isn't the only reward. Also, gaming is big on the riverboats down South. If it comes upstate, we are situated well, even if we moved out of town to a larger place. Why the Mansion, counselor?"

"Truthfully, I think it's because its style is such a success. We don't know the numbers, but from all appearances, it must be highly profitable. And yes, we have thought about the gambling issue. With the Mansion in place, we might be able to inspire a legislative change of heart that gaming should not all stay down south and out of the state's capital. We think that is something that can only be made uncomplicated by native Mississippians and that it would benefit our slow economy. It would be good for the state and its people. Let's say we are public spirited."

"Nicely put, counselor. What about a possible partnership? We stay in and partner up if gambling comes to pass."

"We thought about that too, Rosario, but put it aside. It's our prerogative not yours. Mississippians are a close lot. They like doing business with their own kind. Don't take offense, but they don't cotton much to outsiders. There's nothing new about that. I am afraid it's not in the cards."

Rosario knew now the lawyer was slick. He had it all thought out. He had an answer for everything without hesitation. It was plain that it was a takeover, a buyout. Goodbye, Frenchman.

"Who are your clients, Ross?"

He smiled.

"Rosario, that's why we use lawyers. I can't tell. Some people might have a lot of money. If you knew who the principals were, it might make the deal more costly or problematic. Using a lawyer out front to do the deal is not uncommon, Rosario."

"Well, as you say, Ross, we are all different. It's not French style. We are main-a-main and the lawyers do the paperwork. It's your choice. If we do set a price, we don't want to hold paper, as you say. If we are coming out, we need to be paid out in full. It's a natural business thing to do to talk about the terms of the deal."

"Certainly, cash on the barrelhead as we say. Our thought too."

"What is your thought on timing?"

"I would think no more than a few weeks to cut the deal and finalize the paper. Down here, we move quick when we move. I would say paid out and closed in a month either side of a week, more or less. Not much really to do to close it."

"What about my staff? They have made a commitment coming on board. Do they get contracts or an established work period going forward?"

"Good question, Rosario. I hadn't thought that out. Normally what happens is that we would interview them. After that, we look at the costs and then return to profit and pick and choose. No promises."

"Well, that's a problem for me, Ross. I made commitments to them if they keep theirs to me, and they have. My word is all I have. I'm not pulling the rug out from underneath them. To me, that's not business."

"I'm sure we can work that out to your satisfaction, Rosario."

They both knew that doing so would be at big cost. Contracts made a solid commitment to the help. Rosario had heard enough and spoken it though. He knew that they were hell-bent on taking him out, no matter how steep the hill. The only question was who they were and what did they have to do with the murders? Why did they want him gone?

"What about my future and my opening again elsewhere?"

"That's fine, Rosario, but not in Mississippi. We need a noncompete clause for the whole state just in case we do get gambling. You're very creative, and we don't want the competition."

"Julie and I will talk it over and give you an answer. I don't say yes or no, but if there is no job security built in for my people or Julie says no, then that's our answer."

"All clear, Rosario, but don't be too long at it. Just a few days please."

"Have a good evening both of you, and enjoy the rest of your dinner."

Rosario and Julie were up, and their chairs were removed at once. He left and she went back to rounds. Nothing else was said. Thinking and planning time was back again for both sides on the game board.

CHAPTER TWENTY-FOUR
Rough Rider Room

Julie had fully exhausted herself, raking her brain to find Rosario a way to the information he sought. *Almost desperately,* she thought. She wanted to help and earn her hero's badge by figuring it all out before anyone else did. She knew that she needed to summon up her womanly instinct to get the bottom of it all. The problem was that she wasn't hitting the right notes mentally. The puzzle wasn't falling in place for her, and failure was taking its toll and wearing her down.

It wasn't something she could fight. She just had to keep going plodding along until it meshed and she thought she had it. So she did, looking at the problem from all sides, studying what she thought were common issues.

Days later, she thought she might have her solution developed far enough for an effective program to gather the information Rosario wanted. Rosario was not the key. He didn't know the answer, and it had nothing really to do with him. He hadn't been on the American scene long enough to be a player. He had just been convenient to fill the role of the needed sacrificial lamb. His conviction was orchestrated, and he knew that he had never bumped Vickie Trucker, Miss Bump-and-Testify. She had put him down for the conviction count. Judge Stittin was right about it. The case had been nothing until she had shown up at the bitter end. It had been no happenstance but part of the game plan to stick it on Rosario, shielding the real killer so any further search would end. It was not nice, but it was certainly smart.

These people were clever and certainly of influence and probably money. That led her to think that those behind the cover-up were as much to blame as the killer was because they shielded him (or her), who could not do it himself alone. Why did she not yet understand? It must be the killer's friends, parents, or lovers. That was beginning to make some sense. But why kill two children and a preacher's wife just to orchestrate a cover-up at Rosario's expense? It didn't fit. She reasoned that first the killings happened, and only after disclosure to the movers and shakers did they cover up their conspiracy, shielding the killer and putting it on Rosario instead. The timeline of events needed to be divined. Her version played out neatly without forced thoughts or improbable theories.

No one had expected Rosario to come back to Jackson, let alone open the Mansion, surprising the guilty for sure because they did not know what exactly he was up to. It was his move on them in their own backyard. It was his play to draw them in, and to her mind, it would be irresistible not to succumb.

Anyone guilty of these events would be compelled to come closer at least to access the threat of Rosario and his abilities. It was not a casual undertaking. He was complex enough and smart. He merited close watching on a regular basis. They would have to keep up with him before he outsmarted them, knocked them down and out for the count. The guilty had to protect themselves and keep watch, or it would all fail in the end. Rosario would lay them out, exposed and caught. The time had come when they were stressed out that they were trying to pay him off to go away. They would take over the Mansion and say so long to Rosario. If they thought that he would be bought off, they were not very clever and misperceived him. They were being forced into action, and pressured responses usually led to mistakes. The stakes were building, and everyone wanted to win the pot.

Taking an intellectual step aside to look at the whole game board using her known facts to date, Julie decided that the answer lay in the regulars. One or more of them were the watchers who got inside the Mansion to watch over Rosario. She had a long way to go yet to isolate them and separating the wheat from the chaff.

Years ago in college, she had taken an American history course that focused on the Old West. In the cattle droves that helped build out the newly acquired Western states, the herders moved their stock to market at great distance, often with a hundred men or more. Most of them were camp followers in chuck wagons who supported the far fewer numbers of men who were the real drivers, the rough riders. They did the hard work, moving thousands of head of cattle for twelve hours or more a day on both horseback and foot, bringing in the stragglers. At night at camp, the rough riders did not work. The followers bedded the horses, cooked the meals, and catered to the rough riders who were resting up for another full day in the saddle. They were catered to in every way.

She would wall off the back two thousand feet of the restaurant and put in a separate bar and tables for her regulars (her rough riders) and feed them in their new private space if they wanted. Only established regulars to date would come and go with their own entry card. There would be hosts and hostesses to keep them company and to eat or chat with them, sharing their thoughts and maybe finally their secrets, she hoped. She would handpick the help some from the existing staff and some from the outside. There would be a charge for their company for the evening, just like in Japan and much of Asia. It would be refined and not common. Tipping would be allowed but not for intimate liaisons. Sexual adventures were not the purpose; intimacy at a distance without particular regard to gender would be the order of the day. All other amenities would remain the same.

No new members would be allowed. Julie was sure the guilty she sought were already existing regulars. It was unnecessary, confusing, and not about making even more money Rosario didn't need. It could only slow the selection process down, and time was already up evidenced by the buyout energy. Yes, she would build the Rough Rider Room. It would be a place of ever-changing themes to keep the regulars interested and off guard.

She needed Rosario to go with the program and to put in his ideas and agree to fund the moderate makeover needed in the rear floor space. Otherwise, he could veto it, and she would keep on thinking, even though she was certain it was the cleverest way in with the least suspicion.

Thinking about it more, she realized that the Rough Rider Room had one other strength. If they moved on it at once, it would not take more than a week to put in place, especially if they hired a big enough crew to work from early in the morning until dinnertime. Most of what they needed was already included bathrooms, access to the kitchen, a natural space for the bar and back stairs to the quarters on the floors above, already improved with the elevator that Rosario could use to come and go.

Moving forward with these plans was in part answering the buyout questions. It showed that they weren't all that ready to go. There would be no easy selling out, unless of course, Rosario saw a good reason to do so, including at a very stiff price. Maybe they could play the buy and sell game well enough to open and get the goods of information they sought and still stick the buyers with an outrageous price as they went out the Mansion door they no longer needed. Let's say they became rough riders themselves, riding off into the sunset.

CHAPTER TWENTY-FIVE
Surprise, Surprise

Stephanie was up late but not idle. She was usually off the floor by midnight, because she started earlier than most, doing her details for incoming nightly regulars and other guests from midafternoon. She had broken her shift at ten thirty p.m. leaving word for the others to reach her if any real problems arose.

She grabbed a pot of hot coffee black from nearby, needing its caffeine and went back to the small locked record room that contained the daily servers' and valet take-home reports with the backup logs for the daily front door videos referencing the days of prior visits of Grace and her lawyer friend. They existed in hard form and not microfiche, so they had to be pulled by the discs for the days in question once the computer was searched for the dates any named guest had been in. They could have had a better system that was more interfaced, but the original purposes had not been to sort out specific information for any particular use. It was more the notion of collecting it to see what it led to.

She sat, drank, and thought about her earlier research about the lawyer's drink. In the first few weeks, they had not kept records, and there were no videos yet of the guests. Ross Gillmore II, Esq., was listed as a guest in that opening period according to the reservation book, but her earlier drink information had been from his second of four visits. She had not checked his third and fourth visits, because there had been no reason for it. Rosario had only asked her about his arrival drink for that night of a whiskey sour, which came from the first record.

She checked it again. It was the same as earlier—his name, whiskey sour, visit two. She had made no mistake. She checked visits three and four; the drink was a gin martini, just like that night not whiskey sour. She stood back from the computer only after she took down the disc locations of the video tapes for all three visits. It took her only two minutes to pull all three. She saw the tapes. She ran them again after finishing her review of tape four. She thought that she would run them again but wondered what for. They were not going to change.

The entries had been correct. He didn't drink whiskey sours but instead neat gin martinis just as shown and reported on his third and fourth visits. The man in visit two drank whiskey sours, and he was of the same name, but he was not the same person. He had used the man's name, which was now quite clear. He had passed himself off as the lawyer. He had come in with a female guest. They had arrived late for their dinner, been seated, eaten, and gone. Nothing else of interest had been recorded by the server.

She watched all three tapes: the one reproducing his image and the two later ones of that evening's guest with Grace. She let the computer print two stills of him from each—one for her and one for Rosario. She explained it all in a brief note to Rosario and put them in a large envelope, which she sent up to one fourth floor at once with a busboy. It was only twelve thirty a.m., but she went to her room because her shift was over. She did not expect to hear from Rosario, but she wanted to be onsite if he did have questions.

She was tired. She's lost her adrenaline rush from earlier when she feared that she might have made a mistake. She was glad that she had proved it linked to visit two. The drink was right. The man was wrong, because of the stolen identity. She was no longer pumping hormones, and it had left her feeling flat and empty. She lay down, wondering what Rosario was thinking and drifted off to sleep, though not as easily as usual.

CHAPTER TWENTY-SIX
Getting Somewhere

Rosario was still wide awake and nowhere near ready for bed. He knew it was too innocent an error and that something was clearly afoot. It was what that he did not know. He opened Stephanie's package at once. Identity theft was not new. He was fairly sure already that that was what had occurred before he looked at the photos. One presidential candidate in the last election had been caught using his friend's identity to cover his trysts with the woman who had birthed his child. Maybe it was a Southern man's trick. *Trick or not, it doesn't seem to be very foolproof,* he thought.

He wondered if the real Ross Gillmore II, Esq., knew. Thinking about it, he decided that he did not. If he had, it would be unlikely that he would risk coming in tonight in the flesh, even if he did not know about the tapes. His name was distinctive. He was a governor's son, and it's possible he might have had his cover blown by a server if he were not the same governor's named son who had been in before. Rosario reasoned that, even so, they must know each other. The mystery man in visit two was likely Gillmore's undisclosed client. Mr. Whiskey Sour would be the money man and the killer or his friend.

There was light at the end of Rosario's tunnel. His moth trap, the Mansion, had worked its magic. Only a little more research was needed before the penalty phase could begin. Someone had to know the mystery man. If Ross Gillmore II, Esq., was his errand boy, then he was surely a man of means and influence to engage such high-powered legal help. He was certainly well-known about Jackson even if not to him. But now Rosario had his picture. It was not the best image—it had been taken at some distance by the camera from above the covered car portico in dim light because of the overhang—but it was still clear enough, especially with a magnifying glass.

Like Stephanie and in part due to her focus on the two different men, Rosario had paid no attention to the woman so far. Now he passed his magnifying glass over her. This woman was overdressed for a night out in Jackson. She looked like she belonged on the red carpet at an LA awards event. She was all done up. He brought it closer and studied her features closely as though he was going to cut a rough diamond. Then he exercised his mind, trying to make his brain tissue computer of memory focus on the last trial day. The witness had been plainly attired, looking neat but somewhat frumpy. The woman in the picture was fully done up, a visual knockout of attraction. He could not be sure, too much time had passed, but in his distant memory, he felt they could be the same person—Little Miss Social-Pretty meets Little Miss Bump-and-Tell.

He felt he had come full circle. He was now stalking their path and coming close to his unannounced attack of payback. He advanced the weekly meeting to that midafternoon, calling down to Julie to tell her only of the new date to be set up by her with the other three.

He went to bed but did not sleep until hours later. He had a lot to think about, but he did so in the darkness with a gun. He was sure he had discovered the evil he sought.

CHAPTER TWENTY-SEVEN
Only a Little More Research

Rosario left the Mansion alone with the films in hand by seven thirty a.m. He could have done it at the Mansion, but it would not have been right. Money could not pass hands for this.

The old man was there already, even though it was still well before opening time when Rosario knocked on the shop's glass front door.

"Good morning, Rosario. It's getting warm already, even before spring. Can I get you coffee or something else, please?"

"No, thank you, Mr. Goldstien. That's kind of you, but I had coffee already. How are you?"

"Fine for an old man who gets up too early to earn money I no longer need. I really have nothing else much to do, so I do this. I could travel but it doesn't interest me."

Rosario handed him the envelope. They both knew he had come for something. There was no sense talking more about unimportant matters. There was an old expression in Yiddish. Translated, it went that two Jews could spot each other across a crowded room. The old man had never said it, but his friendship had shown that he knew from the day they met. Rosario was no stranger to him. He would help him all he could if asked from Jew to Jew in a foreign land—Mississippi.

The old Jew didn't need a magnifying glass.

"Fancy friends of yours, Rosario? It seems like strange company for you."

"Friends? No. It's business, but I have to be sure of who they are."

"I know them. Customers both. The lawyer is a big spender, a real dresser like his namesake father. Only tailor-made, nothing off the rack. The other is only off the rack. He's not a cheapskate—of the two of them, he has far more money. He has a lot more, even compared to a governor's son. Ask me what you need to know, Rosario. I don't think it's about who spends what on their clothes."

"Mr. Goldstien, do you remember the church murders a while back?"

"Rosario, I'm old but not senile. I knew who you were the morning you came in. You can't fool a Jewish haberdasher. You had the Mississippi jail freedom clothes still on. I spotted you right off from the pictures last year in the newspapers. It reminded me of the Dreyfus affair all over again. When all else fails, fry a Jew. No one in their right mind, except a Mississippian, could believe someone arrived a few hours before and killed two children and covered them up. The cross business didn't fit either."

"Who is the other man, and how is he hooked up to the lawyer?"

"He is second generation too, Rosario, actually more. The lawyer is a power man, not really so much a lawyer as an influence broker. He is more of a fixer, but not in a corrupt sense. You go to him to get what you want. He tries no cases but still sits at the top of his father's firm and takes care of problems you can't resolve in court. He knows all of his father's cronies and pushes their buttons with money or vice, getting what he wants by keeping their secrets still secret. It's like bribery, but they don't get paid. He keeps them safe. He is more like an old South godfather. He has some rules, but they are all his. If somebody needs something, he is the dog Rover to bring home their bone—at top dollar of course. He doesn't quit easy or back off. You don't get up early in the morning to beat him, Rosario. Once he crosses your path asking what for he wants, you never go to sleep to best him."

"The other man?"

"He is the worst of the worst that Mississippi has to offer. He does what he wants and when he wants and to whom he wants. He's Klan—Mississippi hard-ass redneck-as-it-comes Ku Klux Klan of the third generation. His father was a top dog too; he was Mississippi's grand wizard, but no one wants that job any more. They got the ACLU civil rights boys, who I'm glad to say are Jewish lawyers, suing them all the time. The smart cockroaches stay out of the light, letting the fools say they run the show."

"How does that lead to money? Power, I understand."

"His grandfather married a woman who was old Mississippi, herself a hater. Her family owned a successful group of funeral parlors in the state. Her husband used his pulpit of hate to spoil the competition and attach to people who wanted to share the Klan's mystique while they brought their dead for decades to his homes. The family prospered and bought land, malls, and stone quarries. They started a bank forty years ago. In a poor state, they are among the richest families bar none. Money coupled with the Klan heritage makes the family top dog. I don't know, but since they are about the same age, I bet this twosome are good friends and have been in league with each other since they were kids."

"What is our friend's name?"

"Luther Helms III."

"Does he have family?"

"He does, what is left of it, as best I know. He has a younger wife by maybe ten years, but rumor has it they don't mix well now. Luther is too much around town and putting it in her face—no discretion. He had three children with her, but two, a boy and a girl, are dead. The third is the youngest and not too old. Rumor has it he is odd—not firm in the head, maybe abused, and a druggie."

"Anything else I should know, you think?"

"Not really, Rosario."

"Do you know the woman in the pictures?"

"I don't dress women, Rosario. I can tell you the woman with our friend the lawyer in both pictures is his wife. She comes to help sometimes when he is fitted or to pick out color or fabrics. She is a smart one and kind. She does a lot of charity work, just a plain old good woman who makes him look better, even if it's not true."

"How about Helms' wife?"

"I don't know her, but even still. She is much too young even to be his wife. I'm told the wife is a drinker and aging early. Not the same woman at all, but I have never seen her. This one looks too happy to be his wife."

"What can I do for you, Mr. Goldstien?"

"Nothing but hear advice. Stay away from these people if you can still, if it's not too late already. If you have to dance with them, get yourself some good help. You're going to need it. The best bet would be to pull out and leave Mississippi, but I doubt you'll do that. If you need anything, get to me day or night. Stay safe, safe as you can. Watch out. Take precautions, and don't—whatever you do—underestimate how far these two will go to get what they want. It would not be clever, and you don't look stupid to me. Not hardly."

Rosario thanked him and left. Nothing more was said. Nothing more needed to be spoken. Both men knew it.

CHAPTER TWENTY-EIGHT
Moving Quickly

The weekly meeting opened a day early upstairs. It took a different form from usual; it was more show-and-tell. Rosario showed them his archive and told them who the men were and about the offer to buy the Mansion. They told him about food and guns at the farm, about when the Rough Rider Room would be finished as the regulars at day's end could be treated like cattle drivers with their whims cater to while they sat back and relaxed and be politely and subtly interviewed.

Julie didn't want to speak up; she wanted to be sure first. She excused herself briefly and went down to the record room and searched the computers for the service records for Helms. There were many hits about Mrs. Helms as a dyed-in-the-wool full-time regular and latent drunk. She either came alone or with other customers her age but never her husband. She was a free spender who never wanted to hear the prices. She was in two to three times a week or more, but usually more toward the end of the week. She was always polite, and the servers liked her. The records said her family was in the funeral business. Even without a "III" after her own name, it was clear that she was Mrs. Luther Helms.

In four months, she had been in more than thirty times. At the start, they had regularly taken her and her car home. Now she was dropped off by a house worker or she came with a friend. Nightly, she was taken home when she was ready, most often at closing time and no longer sober. She talked openly to the staff and drivers on the way home, including about personal things. The reports of the college kid drivers noted it all. There was no mention, however, of her children, her husband, or that her younger boy and girl had died. She did not seem ready to discuss these topics. Of the twenty trips home reported, two of Mrs. Helms' drivers thought she might be getting personal, coming on to them. It had happened with other guests, including some of the men. It was something servers reported but didn't act on if they wanted to keep their jobs.

Before shutting down the computers, Julie assembled a printout of the reports on Mrs. Helms. When she described her to the staff on hand before rejoining the meeting, they all knew Mrs. Helms and liked her. Since she did not come in with her husband, they did not link her up to him by name, although many staffers knew no more of who he was. No one thought she was a plant who was spying on them. They thought Mrs. Helms didn't seem to have the energy for it and was not coy. She talked too much about herself, putting no questions to them or even to Rosario, who had greeted her as a regular almost every night she was in.

On the strength of only Julie's good homework, Rosario approved moving forward with the Rough Rider Room on the schedule they had projected. He thought it was worthwhile, even if was only done to loosen up Mrs. Helms. He also thought it was a good reply to the buyout offer to show the buyer it would not be easy. He gave Julie all of the credit for seeing the room's usefulness in this way. He had missed it. It would up the price and help stiffen his terms.

He talked about the helicopter purchase designed to spice up the Mansion's luster with some real flash. Kroper said no; it was too over the top and let the enemy know of their exit plan if they had to cut and run. Kroper knew the air. He was a light aircraft twin engine–licensed pilot able to fly a large Cessna that would hold up to ten people in all.

He had been with Frenchy when they picked out the farm, and Kroper had approved it because of its airfield readiness. The prior owner had moved his runners by air transport from time to time and had a blacktopped 2200-foot runway. It wouldn't hold a jet, but it would take a big Cessna fitted for cargo or people.

Louis could also fly, if need be, and had before, even if he had no pilot's license. When he had been in the remotest places of the world in the legion, no one had cared about credentials as long as he made it up and down without crashing. He was mostly a single-engine man, but he could handle twins and had. Louis wasn't up to Kroper's training, and he didn't have the hours in twins, but he could get them airborne, routed, and landed. What else was needed as long as he could fly it?

Louis kept speaking up on Kroper's side. Both of them could easily handle a single engine, and it could easily hold six—one more person than needed. Kroper and he would be up front piloting, and the three others would be in the back, balancing out the rear. A single engine would fit in the farm's garage, where it would be out of sight and out of harm's way. It would cost little and had the same or maybe a little better range Rosario's idea for a helicopter while being harder to spot and easier to put down.

It finally proved to be a nondiscussion. It made sense. Rosario told them to buy one. Kroper told him no again; it was a waste of money and had disclosure problems. They needed to lease one. That way, the plane would stay registered to the owner and not them, and its numbers if checked even in flight on a computer would not come back to them or a Mississippi address, if they leased from out of state. Kroper's piloting license was not form France but from Germany, so he could lease the Cessna without it coming back to them so quickly. At best, it would take days to sort out the lease operator.

Kroper would need a fuel source onsite at the farm, and it would take much too long for an approved tank site to be installed with all the spill and contaminant permits needed to approve it. His solution was to do what people did in the Third World. It was quicker and cheaper, and they would have no delivery trucks coming in, telling everyone they had an airplane. They would buy a damaged rubber-lined tanker for cheap. They needed it lined to prevent weather changes—even slight ones—from letting in water vapor by perspiring through the inner steel of the tank, watering down the fuel, and spoiling it. They would hand pump from the bottom drain to fill the plane when it was drawn up close. They could put the tanker in the garage too, as long as they kept the windows opened enough to vent.

Rosario told them to put it all together as soon as they could, but discretely, and to bring it all to the farm themselves to avoid gossip or prying eyes. He agreed to a smaller single-engine aircraft. They weren't taking hostages, he thought, and room for six was enough. He hoped they would never need to cut and run, but he knew it would be better to have a way out to be fully prepared.

Cuba was the spot. He told Frenchy to see who they knew who was still down in Cuba. Kroper could arrange with them to get all of them emigrated to Cuba. He could see who had a field to land, who could get them visas, and how to pull the strings now to get it done.

He also asked Louis and Julie to sketch out the Rough Rider Room and its furnishings on their recent as-built Mansion plans. He wanted them to call back the prior workmen they needed to get it going as soon as possible.

Although the meeting had taken less than two hours by the time they filtered out to get down to business, he knew it was too late to call his banker, Hans Gruber, for money. He could call him at home, but it was not an emergency, and that would be impolite. He sent Gruber a text, and called Arnot Sinclair at the Jackson bank, telling him to expect a wire transfer of $250,000 the next day and to let him know when it had been collected into his account. He also asked Sinclair to be his guest soon at the Mansion. He wanted to talk business with him; Sinclair was to tell Sandie to let him know what night he would be at the Mansion. Rosario told him that their discussion would only take a few minutes but that it was fairly urgent.

It was a ploy. Bankers are not lawyers or priests. They have no privilege or obligations of confidence. If Rosario chatted about a possible sale, it would be likely to get around, especially if the bank could posture itself as a player in the deal, by putting it together and earning a hero's badge. It would help to keep the buyers on their toes, even if unsteadily. On the one hand, he was moving forward with his business expansion for the Rough Rider Room, and on the other, he was talking about and planning for sale, which he was leaking in the most natural way—bankers brag. It would keep the buyers at bay, telling them what they wanted to hear and drawing them in.

It wasn't until the next morning that Stephanie told him that the banker had called right back, setting up a table for four for seven p.m. that night. Rosario liked that. He could wait out the weekend, and then reply to Ross Gillmore II on Monday, asking him to meet with them again. This would give the bank the weekend for country club and golf course talk. He could not be sure, but if the cat of disclosure was coming out, it should be by Monday.

It really didn't matter. It was a ploy just like painting the tape on the stock market. It had no downside, so he might as well just play the game. He had put his chips down already. Now it was down to being poker-faced while they tried to outmaneuver him, thinking it was happening behind his back. Time would tell.

CHAPTER TWENTY-NINE

Hustling

It was early Saturday morning, and the Mansion was already hustling and bustling—busy, busy, busy. The building plans had already been modified albeit in pencil; the building crews were onsite; and trucks were bringing in lumber, supplies, hardware, and paint. The kitchen was open early to serve coffee for the nearly thirty tradesmen, electricians, plumbers, carpenters, sheet rockers, locksmiths, brick layers, painters, trimmers, and finally design artists, who would paint Rough Riders on the lintel above the electronic card pass entrance. It was a little past nine a.m., and Julie and Stephanie were coordinating the whole production and seeing to the men's food and other needs.

All of the workmen were getting time and a half every day, and they knew the order of the build-out. No permits were necessary, because only existing interior space was being modified. The walls were staying in the back and rear and being studded out already. The high-pitched whine of the lumber saws was already at full blast as workmen cut the wood to hold the sheetrock that would come next. The front entrance with a double-wide electric door done up as a corral gate was being fabricated onsite in the interior large work area; it would be set in the moment the front walls were place. The work would continue throughout the night, and Frenchy and Louis would take over supervision while the girls rested up for Sunday.

172

Rosario was making four servers—three women and a man—the room's new crew. One of the old bartenders and three new busboys were coming on board for the room too. Other new staff would be interviewed by him on Sunday, all of whom were friends of existing employees, who had been contacted by a staffer at Rosario's request for them to reach out to interest their friends to join up. He already had eleven people scheduled for interviews, and they had been faxed or had picked up their employment applications, which were to be sent back by seven p.m. so he could review them later on Saturday night.

Kroper had left the night before, taking a commuter flight from Jackson to Miami and a 727 American connection to Dallas after staying over at an airport hotel. By then, he would have boarded American's daily eight a.m. commuter to Odessa, where he had arranged to see a single-engine expanded Cessna that held eight people. Due to the larger size, it had a large bore engine for a quicker liftoff on a shorter runway and 30 percent greater airspeed, even with greater passenger weight. Before leaving, he had measured the garage to make sure it would fit without any modifications. He delegated to Louis to find a lined tanker shell and get it moved in and filled with aviation fuel for the Cessna's turbine single-engine Whitney and Pratt 600 model. No other accessories were needed. Small planes went to remote places, especially in Texas. They weren't jets but rather of far simpler design, having a ready supply onboard of replacement belts, light, cables, navigations and radio parts, fluids, and two spare tires that a pilot might need to avoid being really stranded in the middle of nowhere.

For the sake of speed, Rosario would have closed Saturday night, but he didn't feel he could. It would break his record of always being open (except on Mississippi's Sunday), and he had his banker coming in and needed to keep on schedule. They had lost about 20 percent of the table space to the construction. Given the usual crowd of weekend regulars, he told Stephanie to trim back the general reservations, assuming that about thirty regulars would show, as usual, on a Saturday night. It would be better to lose a few tables than be overcrowded with poor service.

If worst came to worst and he was flooded, he would use his own dining area for a small party of twelve with regulars only as his guests for the evening. Julie would attend, and it would end no later than midnight. The guests would be picked by him, and no spies would be included. The banker and his three guests would stay downstairs. Ten minutes would be all he needed for them.

While he was busy, he wondered what Helms and his lawyer buddy Gillmore were doing. He did not need to worry, he concluded, because there was little they could do except get physical. The Klan was a nasty group but hardly military. Instead, Klan members were cowards hiding behind sheets and picking on the weak; they were not legionnaires fitted with knives, guns, fists, and a bloodthirsty disposition when it was time to get down.

There was also backup, if needed. The four of them could each summon up five men or more to be onsite in seventy-two hours or less, with more to come if war broke out. The farm could hold them, feed them, and arm them all, if need be. While that was a comfortable thought, he believed it would be unnecessary. It was so unlikely, and he would not call for reinforcements before he knew they were needed. However, safe was better than sorry. When Kroper was back on Sunday night or Monday at the latest, he would have everyone call around to his friends, raising the alert to amber, putting them on standby, and taking measure of who was available and their legionnaire skills.

CHAPTER THIRTY
Painting the Tape

S aturday night was busy with far more guests than expected. Nearly all forty regulars were in, and Stephanie had cut off the reservations at two thirty p.m. with the tables set aside taken. The banker only had three people, but many of the regulars had brought guests, which was both unusual and unexpected. It was not a question of food—there was plenty of that. It was a space problem.

Rosario thought that letting the pressure off by moving a dozen people up to dine with him still would not solve the problem. Julie didn't like that idea either, because it would expose the layout to unknown eyes, maybe leading to disclosure and future trouble. Rosario thought that, if anyone really wanted to know the layout he could have it from a worker. Julie said they didn't really know about how his space was laid out or that his three comrades were routinely in residence and where. They came and went by the private rear elevator that was not exposed to the staff. No one should be wandering around the fourth floor.

Rosario gave in to what he knew was Julie's good advice, which was meant to keep him and all of them as safe as could be. He would err on the side of caution. He had wanted to dine upstairs, in part, because Mrs. Helms was in that evening. If he made her part of the upstairs guests if she was in a drinking mood as usual, he might be able to subtly interview her, gathering any information. Julie's pervasive veto made that a no go, but Stephanie solved the problem. They shut down the dance floor for the night and brought in the tables from the Rough Rider Room. No one was crowded, and no one complained of being short-changed by one night without dancing.

Maybe they should shut dancing inside down for good and put it out on the veranda, with heaters in the cooler months. It would only be impossible in January and February, and that was not much of a loss. Next month, she would try it. The dance space was darker, and maybe the guests would like it, because it would be less of a spectacle than it was in the well-lit dining room. They would mix it all up a little bit, making changes here and there. If it worked, they could cover the veranda the following winter for a few months and run a service bar or maybe put in a small band.

The banker came in at seven p.m. as promised, with three others in his party. One was his wife, and the other two were unknowns. They were introduced as his wife's relatives, who were up from Birmingham, and by all accounts, the women looked to be her sisters. Both of them spoke like "Bammy" natives with that slow, drooling drawl. He owned a few gas stations, and she worked for the post office. It looked like what it was: a family outing well beyond their means on any regular basis. It was a treat as a night to remember. Rosario had ordered a fine 1973 Perrier crystal champagne to be sent over when they came in, and by seven forty-five p.m. when he greeted them, it was liquid history. He told Stephanie to send in another, and she did as he was greeting them.

Rosario wanted to be discreet and asked Sinclair to join him privately for a few minutes, telling his family that he would be back soon enough and before any dinner service. They stepped to a small reserved table for two on the service side of the bar. Pleasantries were exchanged. The barman, Dino, set down bottled water with iced lemon glasses, poured, and withdrew.

Rosario opened, "Arnot, we have already been quite successful here. You must know by the deposits made to our operating account. On a regular night, we are operating overall between fifty to fifty-five percent profit, putting us at a return usually only for bar service. I think by next month, I will have earned back our full opening costs."

"Rosario, I have seen the deposits, and they are generous for a restaurant compared to the others in town. No one is anywhere close to your revenues. I am sure there must be other restaurants in big cities that could match you, but not in Mississippi."

"Arnot, I think, if the style works here, it will succeed elsewhere. I'm thinking of opening in other Southern cities, but the smaller ones—not Atlanta or Miami—some place where you can get a loyal group of regulars and good spenders."

"It makes sense, but who would run the Mansion if you and Julie move on?"

"Well, she could stay and I could relocate, but I think she is part of the success and needs to be with me for it all to work. Also, I think that, together, we are part of the attraction."

"Well, you and she have certainly become local heroes or public personalities for Jackson anyway."

"What is the style in Jackson, Arnot, if I were to sell out? Multiples of earnings? Some say five times profit, and I have heard as high as eight. Also, who should I use to make the deal? I don't need a restaurant broker. I have already been approached by Ross Gilmore and an unknown buyer."

"I would say there is no rule here, Rosario. When a Mississippian sells something, it's all you can get. You can get more if you are financing it by taking back a mortgage."

"No way, Arnot. I want out clean. If it doesn't stay a success with a new owner, I want no risks. Let me know who you think for a seller's law firm and who at it should carry the ball."

"You got it, Rosario. I'll let you know late Monday or Tuesday. Shall I speak to them first?"

"Whatever you think is best, Arnot. You know the way it is here much better than I do. I just want the best price."

"Fine. Here is your confirmation on the last wire deposit from Switzerland, and thank you so much for dinner tonight."

"Enjoy yourself, Arnot, and have fun with your family tonight. It's what the Mansion is all about. You're very welcome, and please say goodnight to your family for me. We are in the middle of construction, and it's taking a lot of my time day and night right now."

"What's the new secret, Rosario?"

"Something for our regulars only, something new. It's sort of an entertainment theme that will keep changing so no one gets bored with us."

"So why build now if you're going to sell soon?"

"I'm staying if I don't get my price, so I might as well keep going. If it works out, then the buyer is so much ahead. If not, I am still on schedule."

"Makes sense. Goodnight, Rosario."

"Goodnight, Arnot, and thank you."

Rosario went off to make his rounds with Julie, visiting all the tables. Arnot went back alone to his table and guests, mulling over what he had been told and trying to calculate how he could benefit.

CHAPTER THIRTY-ONE

Sunday Comes Early

It was no day of rest. The workmen were back before eight a.m., calculating the progress of the night shift and planning how best to move forward. Rosario, Julie, and Stephanie were considering what they needed done for special touches and a few changes as the room progressed. Louis and Frenchy were making phone calls to Cuba and elsewhere, locating legionnaires who might be asked to come on board. Kroper called in and was on his way back from Texas. Louis had located where to get aviation fuel and was still working on a lined holding trailer. Everything was moving forward.

Rosario spent the better portion of the day interviewing the applicants. He hired twelve more servers and six busboys, increasing the staff in service even more inside the Rough Rider Room. All were friends or relatives of existing staff, and he had plenty of second floor space to house them. Training was to start the next day. He liked the fresh new faces and their enthusiasm in joining up. Obviously, those who had gone before them had described his Mansion as a great opportunity, especially for Jackson.

He needed more help, because they had decided to close the dance floor, build out a new location on the veranda, and heat it for a while until warm weather returned. A service bar would be set up, and two of the new arrivals were already trained bartenders. The additional new staff would replace those lost to the new spaces and service the additional dance floor space. It would ease the burden on the existing staff. Even if many were still in training, he planned to be fully staffed by midweek and finished with all construction.

Only Louis went to the farm that day to see to Kroper and help him on arrival. No tanker had yet been found, but he had brought in ten full fifty-five gallon tanks of aviation fuel to be hand pumped into the plane for one fill-up on hand if needed. Kroper knew to come in with a full tank.

Around three thirty p.m. with the sun just beginning to go down, Kroper descended at full speed from the West with his back to the sun, becoming difficult to see but not hear. He assumed that at least Louis was there to watch the show. When he was twenty yards above the main house, he tilted his wings and pulled up his nose full rise, which was only a 30 percent tilt for the Cessna 8. It was no Blue Angel jet able to rise straight up ninety degrees, but Kroper was doing his best to show he had it mastered and had it under control at full performance. He turned hard left, banking into the wind to land on the strip, broke his airspeed to seventy miles per hour, hit the runway only ten yards in, and stopped at about 1,500 of 2,200 feet. He rolled the plane down the rest of the way, and took the right turn just short of the end to circle back to the runway to taxi nearer to the house.

Louis was waving him in and had opened the large double doors of the garage. Kroper came back down nearly the full runway again, exiting onto a ramp on the right that brought him to the garage entrance. The wing span gave him about six feet on either side, and Louis signed that he was well lined up and not too high. If more men were there, he would have been turned around and backed in for direct exit. Given a small incline coming in, two men could push the plane out or pull it out with a truck hitch, but it would take time. If they were hurried, both doors could be electronically opened and the magneto sparked remotely so the engine could warm up quickly enough to take to the runway and get airborne in less than two minutes. It would take five minutes or more if the plane had to be pulled out backwards. There would be no hiding a takeoff, which meant risking engagement or a blocking of the runway, which was still always a risk if the opposition was thinking clearly and managed to get a vehicle in.

Kroper jumped out the cabin door and gave Louis a fine legionnaire comrade hug. With each man smiling, they backed up on the wing, stepped down, and in through the cabin door back into the plane. Kroper did all the talking, telling Louis what flight features were available, seating him in the copilot's seat.

The next day and thereafter until Louis was comfortable with it, they would practice exiting the garage with two men only as well as takeoff, landing, and in-flight management, filing up at a different airport before coming in at day's end. Each night, they would train for moonlight flight. Nothing was being left to chance.

On day two, Louis stocked the plane with dry foods, prepared goods for the microwave, water, and juices—all stored in the built-in cabinets. Fresh water for the small toilet and sink was hosed into the ten-gallon container. Nothing else was needed but medical supplies. There were enough of those in a large suitcase to be carried into the cabin with another large open-top canvas bag that contained small arms. Several semiautomatic long guns and a cut-down double-barrel twelve-gauge shotgun were permanently racked inside the cabin.

Their exit plan was fully ready if needed.

CHAPTER THIRTY-TWO

Opening Night and Beyond

The Rough Rider Room was to be a constantly changing theme from week to week. The regulars were paying regular price and half more just to visit. It would be interesting to see who, if anyone, dropped out and would be easily replaced by other guests who were coming more often to work up to regular status.

Rosario and Julie were part of both worlds of the Mansion, attuned to both regular and casual guests. The opening week in the Rough Rider Room, given its name, was the trail driver's theme itself, and the servers and busboys and barmen inside were decked out in full western cowboy gear. There were cowboy hats for any of the room's guests who wanted to join in. On the opening night of each new week, it would always be a surprise theme, but by the next night, the regulars would spread the news to their friends. So by the second night, the regulars were coming in dressed like cowboys or whatever else was going on. It was intimate and broke the social ice; the guests who knew each other for most of their lives were actually relating to each other in a festive mood. It was far more than just having dinner. It was Hollywood in Jackson, with a party every night. No one was dropping out, but instead guests were posturing their best to get in. By week's end, it was the talk of Jackson. The new must-have membership; they must be seen there.

The regulars were coming in even earlier and spending more. Their doors opened at six a.m., and a special rear entrance was improvised to keep these customers from coming through the main dining room, if they wished to avoid being seen in their costumes.

On Monday of the next full week, a new creation of the regulars developed. They came already in costume, trying to guess the week's theme by coming in as pilots, nurses, doctors, police, firemen, and endless other creations. It had become a theater of gaiety. One of its prime shakers and movers was Mrs. Helms, who was not missing any party. She became a regular's regular and was in attendance nightly. Since she could easily afford it, she outdid the others in dress, expense, and keeping company with the staff, who were there to help the party along and, if selected, to sit, drink, or eat with guests if there was a hostess house charge, with tipping both allowed and expected. The cost certainly kept the meek of wallet out, but those who partied spent in the manner they should. As they drank and ate, they bared their secrets and disappointments. These were faithfully reported in the hosts' daily guest notes.

Rosario had been carefully easing into a nightly dialogue with Mrs. Helms, greeting her at first only for a few minutes on arrival. Days later, he took to joining her as the evening progressed after she had eaten and enjoyed her host's companionship. The host would leave on Rosario's arrival but not mingle with other guests, ready to return when Rosario excused himself. No one else was present when they spoke. Mrs. Helms had given up on bringing or meeting guests, preferring instead the host's company.

As the nights passed, her conversations with Rosario increased in length, with disclosure of the true nature of Mrs. Helms' life and its many disappointments. The discussions were in the nature of releasing a life burden without any personal interest by her in Rosario. Julie also dropped by from time to time, with and without Rosario present, and it became plain that Mrs. Helms was the Mansion's prime benefactor. Nothing seemed amiss or devious.

CHAPTER THIRTY-THREE

The Past Begins to Be Revealed

The second full week was themed doctors and nurses, so some had guessed it right. On the second night, Mrs. Helms was in, looking like a Mississippi redo of Florence Nightingale who had been from a prosperous family long ago. Unlike the other guests who had dressed up from a downtown store that sold hospital uniforms and shoes, Mrs. Helms was not so modern. It was a tribute to her own sense of theater and acting. She had well researched all things from a picture of Nightingale in the Crimean War and had her tailor put together an authentic-looking uniform of the day with its dark blue and stark white colors, complete with cap and service badge. As before, she stood out from the rest and received many compliments for her obvious nod to historical accuracy without regard to expense. It pleased her and set her at ease; it gave her a theme of her own to repeat weekly. It was good fun, and she was hardly too old to seek its humor. There had been little enough of it in Jackson for her before the Mansion. She was no longer feeling suffocated by still hidden prior events and disappointments.

For that second Monday night opening, Rosario came down and went directly to the Rough Rider Room to greet his most valued regular guests. He passed by Mrs. Helms, saving her for last as a matter of her status and knowing he would sit with her later as did she. After finishing inside, he worked the regular dining room with Julie, and it was functioning smoothly with the new help.

At about eight thirty p.m., Julie and Rosario returned to the regulars, and joined Mrs. Helms, who was alone at the moment. Rosario complimented her dedicated attire, saying she made a perfect Florence Nightingale. Julie agreed politely and retired, as she and Rosario had agreed earlier. With the pleasantries done, Mrs. Helms replied that she could be a "helpful nurse to a needy doctor like you."

It was, he thought, a knowingly provocative comment, especially the doctor part, which told him that she knew a secret or two about him. She wanted to tell him something that she knew was important to him. He knew at once that the ice had cracked, and he was about to be enlightened finally.

Still taken aback but drawn awake as thought with a cold shower, Rosario replied in a calm voice, "How so?"

"Rosario, you didn't come back to Jackson to build a successful restaurant, I think."

"Maybe not, Mrs. Helms, but then why else?"

"To balance the scales of justice, of course, Rosario. Let's say, cure the problem of year past, doctor."

"Why would I want to do that? I served my time."

"Certainly, but for what, Rosario? You never said you were guilty, and we know you weren't."

"I know it, but how do you know for certain, Mrs. Helms?"

"Know what, Rosario? About the murder or your reasons for coming back?"

"Both or either."

"Rosario, women are not well regarded here, but that does not mean we are not clever. We have a way about us, and we go about learning things."

"I am certain of that, and I have never fostered any beliefs of female inferiority and certainly not to you, Nurse Nightingale. If anything, my beliefs in the power of women are most complimentary, especially when compared to the crudeness of men."

"Rosario, words alone need not be the only medium. Obviously, you returned, let's say to the scene of the crime, for good reason. You started the Mansion, predictably to help the cause. Jackson folk came forward, and you watched them. I came so I could be watched and watch you, making up my own mind."

"About what?"

"About you and what needed to be done."

"Done about what, Mrs. Helms?"

"Why you, of course, Rosario … done about you."

"How so?"

"Rosario, among the privileged, Mississippi is really a small community. You might be considered a threat to some, even if they were not yet awake to any danger."

"So how did you sort it out?"

"You watched me, and I watched you, Rosario. I am not one for others' advice. I made up my own mind."

"To what conclusion, Mrs. Helms, if I may ask?"

"We wouldn't be taking finally if my agendas needed to stay hidden any longer, young man."

Rosario smiled. He had not been called that since his school days. He had been "young man" to the headmaster the day he had learned his parents had died. Here it was again, but now perhaps it was a good omen.

"So what did you discover, my clever nurse?"

"All about you, of course, Rosario. Your mystery background all the way back home to France."

"To what conclusion?"

"Not really the right word, Rosario. Facts are not really conclusions but only lead, at best, to logical deductions. I sought information."

"Successfully, I presume?"

"I went to a friend who traced your travel back to France. It seemed it ended in a cold trail, but not so really. I learned from the warden's family—actually his son—that you are an accomplished doctor. No one gave you up, Rosario. It was only a child talking about what he had heard or knew, innocence itself. My sister's husband is uncle to the boy on his mother's side."

"Small Mississippi world indeed, Mrs. Helms."

"After you opened in the fall and I came regularly, I met your French friends, Rosario. Clearly not Mississippians, and I saw you and Julie. I made up my own mind about who is who and the why of it. Obviously, the men are here for you in every way—let's say they're your comrades. Julie is the smart, local touch. Let me tell you, Rosario, just don't let her slip through your fingers. Big mistake. Give it up if you have to, but don't lose her. Not worth it, Rosario. She's a gem."

"We agree, for sure. I will heed your advice as best I can, but I'm only half the story."

"Maybe you should talk to her about it if you haven't already, Rosario. Money is one thing. Companionship is quite another."

"Thank you, Mrs. Helms."

"Not hardly, Rosario."

"So that's what you came to tell me?"

"Not exactly, Rosario. It is simply an obvious observation to not let any ideas of payback or revenge blind you to what you have developed. Try to balance your own scales of good and bad. No, there is much more, Rosario. Your friends all have an obvious sign, an upside-down cross. Not always easy to see at first. You have none. It was puzzling."

"To what end?"

"Several weeks ago I went to Marseilles, France, where you flew in from. A few people know the sign of the French foreign legion re-enlisted men. Your picture helped. The city is full of men who have left the corps. Some know your picture, doctor. All liked or, let's say, respected you. I had no reason to learn more there. I rely upon my own instincts."

"With me, you mean?"

"Yes, of course. That's what we are doing now."

"So what am I to do to drag it out of you? Just ask? Have the comrades give you a going over? Beg. Sell you the Mansion?"

"I'll take the 'just ask,' Rosario. Nothing more really, doctor. You paid the price."

"So who did it? The murders, I mean?"

Mrs. Helms looked at him hard and fastened her eyes on his. Long seconds passed, but no answer came. It was a moment of truth, like Caesar crossing his armies into Rome past the Rubicon; it was a single moment of opportunity taken or lost for good.

"My only surviving child, Rosario."

Now it was his turn to lay back and think about what to say next.

"I'm sorry, Mrs. Helms. I never thought … "

"Not as sorry as I am, Rosario. You couldn't be."

"Why?"

"Robert lost … we, the Helms family, lost his brother and sister about five years ago. Some say by accident, but I still don't know for sure. I'm not finished with that yet. Robert was the oldest. He was still only twelve at the time. He was there, but his mind is blocked and now for good, I think."

"What happened?"

"They were seven and eight, Mary and Peter. Their father, the big shot wizard, had taken them to a Klan weekend. These Mississippi Ku Kluxers are hard drinkers. Night tempers flared, and there was shooting. One bullet killed them both. Robert was in between them. It missed him, but he was covered in blood."

"That's horrible," Rosario said. His own young grief flashed through his mind, and he stated his own innermost feelings truthfully in a voice from the heart.

"Robert was never strong in the head. Physically well off but not mentally. All that Klan exposure did him no good. After that, he kept getting sicker and sicker. I wanted a doctor to treat him, but Mr. Helms didn't want the boy or the Helms family name branded with mental illness."

"So he kept getting worse, no doubt."

"Pursued by demons until the killings. God talked to him and told him what to do, and he did it. After the murders, there was nothing left of him, just any empty mindless blank in flesh and clothes. He was emotionless and speechless."

"Now where is he?"

"Locked up, Rosario—physically and in his mind. He was institutionalized involuntarily, and he is not leaving. He's had a frontal lobotomy to fix his mind against further crimes and disability. Mentally, he is twelve years old and would never stand trial. He is a dead end. Your dead end, Rosario, and my dead end, which we share."

"Was he alone?"

"Yes."

"When did you know?"

"The same night. He came home on his bike. He had their blood on him. Word of the killings was already the night's gossip. I took care of him until we put him away. Mr. Helms took care of the problem. Took care of you, I should say. To save you asking, he didn't talk to me about it. I gave no permission."

"I suppose he needed none."

"It's not an excuse for me. I'm saying I had no hand in it. I could have come forward to clear you. I didn't know then if Robert could get better or even stand trial. I have lost two children to violent deaths, and knowing Robert is alive is at least a small victory for a mother. It's not much really, considering his condition. No. I chose him over you, and in the end, it was not much time that Judge Stittin gave you. If you had gotten the book thrown at you, I'm not sure even now if I would have spoken up then or not."

"So why now?"

"Because with his mind fixed and unable to be convicted, it gives me peace of mind. Not for you, Rosario, for your revenge, but for me. I help myself these days, Rosario. My help to you is not to get blinded by hate or to let yourself drown in self-pity and lose out on Julie. Save yourself, Rosario, if you can still."

"Who helped your husband? No one could have done it alone, Mrs. Helms."

"Women aren't let into the working of men's affairs. We only bear children and smile down here. We are the original Stepford Wives, airheads. We're pretty to look at with nothing to say, if we know our place."

"Do you? Seems to me you're well beyond that stupidity."

"Only because I can afford to be, Rosario, but it's still true that Mr. Helms says little or nothing to me, especially these days. We are estranged at best, ever since I lost Mary and Peter to the Klan. It's not Mr. Helms' money that rules the roost here, Rosario. It's Trumball money that started the funeral homes for the Helms family. My family funded their growth. It was strictly business, and we're not Klan folk. Business got good, and our fathers made a marriage match. No love, Rosario, just more business. It was about what the Helms family needed and not the other way around. Now it's over."

"How so?"

"Enough is enough, sooner or later. I'm thinking divorce. Before it was a problem, especially with Robert, but now nothing more will change. We don't need each other anymore."

"What about his support and your lifestyle? You'll miss that."

"No, Rosario. The Trumballs own the land and buildings of the funeral homes, and for now, the Helms family pays no rent because they are my family. That will change when I leave. Trumballs own the malls and the two riverboats and the downstate casinos and hotels. I have no money worries."

"Well, that can ease things. I know."

"Obviously, you must, since you paid your bills here handsomely with Swiss funds. People here gossip a lot, so don't be surprised. It would have been more private if you were a local, but you and Julie have been the subject of chitchat and rumor for months now. It goes with your territory of success. It's part of the price of admission to our society."

"If you need help, just let me know."

"Thank you, Rosario. I'll do that."

"Anything else I need to know?"

"Yes, just the final rumors a woman hears who keeps her ears open and her mouth shut. My holdings in the Trumball family casino business are held in a trust. Our fathers thought it up long ago. How to control me was the main concern. The trustee is a banker but also a Klansman. He too bows to the devil grand wizard. Our Jackson sheriff gets five percent of the profit, as does my husband's whore, Rosario. You remember her, I'm sure. She was the last witness against you. They are quite a couple. Ten percent goes to the family of the children our son murdered. The church mortgage was paid off by us, but the pastor died six months ago, so he is off the payroll, I assume."

"Money does buy everything, it seems—at least in Mississippi. Why doesn't he divorce you and marry her?"

"He can't. The trust was to keep us both in control. It ends if he divorces me. His girlfriend's payments are finished, and the funeral homes need to start paying rent. He can't leave. If I do, it's not clear if my trust can be broken. It gets the rest of the income and ownership of half of one riverboat. The rental monies of the malls and hotels, my sister and I split outright. Altogether, it's a fortune, so I have no need for more large sums, even if the trust might not break."

"Why now? Why not before?"

"Because hate blinds, Rosario, like I just told you. It's what I have learned these last two years. I wanted him to leave, to divorce me, so I could force him to stop the payments to his bitch and the sheriff by his own action. Now I realized I am sinking myself by anger and hate. I need to find my own lifeline again, to move on just like I've told you. Give up the payback."

"I'll think about it."

"That's all you can do, Rosario. You're younger, so maybe it won't take you as long. Let me know if you want to talk about it anytime soon."

Their talk was over. She left early, and he went upstairs early. They both went their separate ways to do the same thing: think about where they were and where they needed to go as well as what roads they would use to get there. Would they choose hate and payback or move on and save their souls? Time would tell.

CHAPTER THIRTY-FOUR
Decision Time

Rosario exercised his mind for several days until the next group meeting. He had tried to resolve it himself, but he could not. He had too many mixed feelings about payback versus turning the other cheek. He was getting nowhere. He thought maybe he should talk it out with Julie to get to the bottom of what she wanted. He wanted to talk it out with her alone, but in a way, he felt that would be selfish regarding his comrades, who had spent so much time and energy helping him. He decided he would put it to them all at the same time and see what they all said after they thought it over.

It took him less than a half-hour to lay it all out for them. The four of them listened. No one spoke; they just listened, nodded, and made eye contact with each other when Rosario mentioned a key point. When he was done, no one spoke up.

Kroper broke the ice. "I think I'll try to start training Mrs. Helms now. She seems ready to gather up her strength to break out."

Julie shot him a glance as though he had betrayed her. She was still his pupil, and she resented any competition. They locked onto each other eyes, staring each other down, and then they broke out in laughter together. It was silly. It was a sign of their bonding that they both reached the same conclusion at once. Helping Mrs. Helms would only strengthen their own bond and move them all toward a showdown, the real conclusion that they all needed.

They talked it over and agreed in part on how to proceed if Mrs. Helms agreed. Nothing would affect the payments being made to the victim children's family from the casino. It was little enough and could never replace the horror of their children's deaths.

Nothing would be done to the Helms boy, Robert, despite his murders. He had not set Rosario up. He was sick, just plain mentally ill, and that went back to the Klan meeting deaths of his siblings. He had been fixed in time at the age of twelve by his brain surgery. His mother was also right; even if it was all exposed, no Mississippi jury would convict him. Robert would also be institutionalized for the rest of his life, hidden away in a private facility, even if the facility had the plushest comfort that big money could buy. He was still locked up forever in his mind and in his body, never able again to come and go alone where and when he chose. No more punishment was due him. No more control over him was needed.

This left Mr. Helms for payback, and he was obviously the origin of the cover-up and the framing of Rosario. It could not have happened without the sheriff's help or without Vickie Trucker, the key bump-and-lie witness. The real question was not who deserved payback but what it should be.

Ever true to his past, Kroper felt that taking them out altogether—disposing of them—would be the quickest and best solution. No one else agreed, and all for the same reason: They had killed no one to date, so killing them would be over the top. It would also make them all killers too. No good could come of that, and it would only be trouble for each of them going forward. It did not balance out with Rosario having lost a little more than a year of his own life. The punishment didn't fit the crime. As they talked it out, Kroper was drawn around to agree.

It was also somewhat confusing. Was Kroper deep down inside himself opting for the death penalty because it would make Mrs. Helms more approachable and vulnerable? Had Kroper thought so far in advance? Despite his superb conditioning, she was still more than a half-generation younger and unlikely, at fifty, to give him natural heirs. What did he really want? How could it be very clear at all to him until he enjoyed a deeper one-on-one relationship with her? It was much too soon to predict. Only time would tell.

After three hours more, it had all been hashed out. There was no perfect game plan, only a focus and an end result. Rosario had reasoned that, in the end, two things were needed: an admission of guilty behavior against him, and deprivation of what they all craved—money.

It was agreed that lying Vickie Trucker was the weakest link. She wanted money and status—respectability. She would not be the first dime-a-dance girl to hit the male jackpot. Mr. Helms had big money and not just a thousand a week. He had status both in the Klan and in Mississippi society due to his wife's family's money. It was not enough for Vickie to get the showboat gambling payoff. She wanted it all and to be a wife of distinction in local society who would be able to live like Mrs. Helms herself. Her own scheming would denounce her to them and make her weak enough to compromise the others, who had promised Rosario. She was the selected road in for payback.

As for Mr. Helms and the sheriff, that would be simple if Vickie gave them up. It would be uncontestable and done quickly. Each would give up the riverboat money. Mrs. Helms would divorce her husband, and the funeral homes would pay rent—at least those that he kept, since they were community holdings to be split between husband and wife in the divorce. He would still not own the land that his were on or have any continued interest in the casinos since the trusts already prohibited it in her favor if they were no longer married.

It was true that Kroper could help by getting closer to Mrs. Helms to help her prepare for when the time to leave her husband was finally at hand. It was coming soon enough. Hopefully, revealing the truth of what he had done to Rosario to Miss Trucker would finish their relationship. This alone would help get Mrs. Helms onto the right track with Kroper's support.

At the same time, everyone knew Mr. Helms could not run the Mansion or keep the help. However, to mask the plan of payback, Rosario would move forward with a plan to sell. The Mansion would not come cheap. Five million would be the price. If Mr. Helms took the bait and had to try to pay for the Mansion without his wife's resources after the divorce started, it would bankrupt him. No way would Vickie stick around to support him.

Generally, it was agreed that this would be the overall plan. No votes were taken, because none were needed.

CHAPTER THIRTY-FIVE
Getting the Proof

Late that same day, Rosario called his lawyer. He told him to communicate by letter faxed to Ross Gillmore II that Rosario would sell the Mansion for an all-cash price of five million, which included the property, business, and inventory "as is" on the day of closing, which would be set as soon as possible but not more than thirty days after contract signing. A million-dollar nonrefundable deposit would be placed in escrow, even if no closing took place due to the buyer's default. A letter of credit was to insure the availability of the rest of the funds in case any dispute about default arose. Once there was such a contract, there would be no backing out. While it had not been confirmed, Rosario remained certain that Mr. Helms was the buyer.

Frenchy was tapped to do research on Miss Trucker. Using her name and address alone, he hacked into the Holtsville IRS tax records to pick up her social security number. It was easier than anyone thought, and he had plenty of experience in getting into government records from his prior intelligence work with the legion. With her social security number, he went next into her banking records and both her American Express and Visa card accounts. He searched her charges for anything relevant, including deposits and her records of the banks on which checks were drawn. He went back to six months before the killings and on down to the present.

He printed out the results and examined the hard copies at his leisure cross-referencing one to the other after he closed down all of his hacking accesses and deactivated his computer key route entry, which he dead-ended at a blind resource he had set up long before in Bogota, Columbia. Even if his entries were picked up, there would be no tracing them farther than Columbia to a site more than ten years old. All anyone would know is that the records had been hacked by an expert. Otherwise, it was a complete dead end them.

A few hours later he had put it altogether and Xeroxed sets of key documents for the others with one extra for Miss Trucker when the time came for confrontation. It proved that her income before the murders was marginal at one thousand dollars per week in child support that was deposited by weekly wire transfer to her bank account; that six weeks after the murder, she received a check for twenty-five thousand dollars, which she deposited to her bank account and had been drawn from the Helms' funeral home account; that two weeks after her testimony, she began to receive regular distributions by check from Biloxi, Mississippi, drawn on the Helms family's casino account (in one year going, they had totaled $180,000 and were being paid in fifteen thousand–dollar installments about once a month); that two days before the murder, she had an airplane ticket to New York City for her and her child. She had spent the week shopping, according to her own credit card charges. She had not even been in Mississippi, let alone bumping into Rosario at the time of the murders. Frenchy did not check with the airline to confirm her travel, because the shop and restaurant bills made it clear enough where she was at the time. He had the goods on her and Mr. Helms, due to the twenty-five thousand–dollar payoff, after which they had become an item. It would be hard for him to shake her off (assuming he wanted to) after the history of his payoffs to her.

Encouraged, Frenchy hacked into the sheriff's bank accounts from his terminal in Bogota, Columbia. No one would be on to him yet, and by the time it got back to him, if it ever did, the search would still have a dead end. There was no way to track him down unless someone did it when he was online and that was both unlikely and too soon. It would still not be easy, as there were three more dead-end routings. The tracker would have to come into each one and know how to enter, when, and the key codes. Finally, he had to have very sophisticated equipment that was available only to a few government intelligence agencies of first-world countries, not one of which would have any interest in such banking entries, even if they were picked up. They looked for specific intelligence information and not simple bank or tax incursions that would lead nowhere except to an isolated hacker with some private agenda.

The sheriff had been a little cleverer—at least it appeared so—in covering his tracks, but not by very much. Like before, he printed out what he found and made Xerox packages for the others, showing his involvement. The sheriff had also received a check from Helms Funeral Home for twenty-five thousand dollars; his had not been deposited but cashed. It had come two days after Rosario was charged with murder. He had no deposit history of monthly payments from the Helms casino. His tax return for the murder year implicated him. Mr. Helms had pinned him down and compromised him. The sheriff had received two 1099 tax payment statements for the twenty-five thousand dollars and the casino profit payments, which obligated him to declare them and pay taxes. Helms was keeping his thumb on him to prevent him from turning against him as a state's witness or blackmailing him. After all, he was not Mr. Helms' girlfriend with thoughts of marriage.

Frenchy gave the others each a package, and a special meeting was set for the next night at dinner time. For the first time, no one would be going down to circulate on the dining room floor. Dinner would be upstairs.

Then Kroper put a question to them. Should they invite Mrs. Helms, asking her to join in with them as repayment for her candor?

Rosario agreed at once, so there was no other discussion. Everyone wanted her on board. Each thought that it was good for them and good for her. She completed the team.

CHAPTER THIRTY-SIX

Moving Forward

By midday, Rosario had confirmation of a deal on his terms, including the letter of credit. No provisions were made for continuing to employ his staff, but Rosario could do that with the sale profits. He was pretty sure he would get the property back sooner or later, so it would be like a Hollywood strike he had read about. The late-night Johnny Carson pundits had paid their writers and production crews to stand by throughout the strike. He would do likewise.

Night came, and the Mansion opened. Stephanie knew that, for the first time, she would be on her own. She had picked a handsome barman, who knew most of the guests, to circulate with her. They were a backup couple in training to Rosario and Julie. They too made a fine-looking pair. No one else yet knew that the Mansion was being sold, and for once the rumors lagged behind the reality of events. The buyer had strictly required that there be no publicity and even forbade any public recording of the contract of sale lest some clever title searcher pick it up by accident.

Rosario's lawyer searched for the buying corporation. It came back to a new incorporation that was only a few days old and had been made by Ross Gillmore II as the buyer's agent. There would be no record of the actual owners. It was much too early for an annual public filing of officers, directors, and shareholders. However, Gillmore was no fool. He was being well paid—a fifty thousand–dollar fee, or five times what it was worth, for a very routine transaction. He intended to do his very best for the grand wizard who had hired him to get it done at once.

The million dollar deposit would give him no source. It would go into Gillmore's law firm's trust account. Its source would be shielded by attorney-client privilege. The letter of credit guarantee for four million dollars in closing monies was another matter. The bank would issue it in the bank's name, but it would do so for a forty thousand–dollar fee the buyer would have to put up the four billion dollars in collateral with the bank or an insurance policy for the amount with another large fee. It would certainly disclose who the buyers were.

Rosario's lawyer asked Arnot Sinclair to call his counterpart at the buyer's bank to find out who the buyer was. By then, the buyer's banker knew of the sale already. If it was going to be revealed, it would not take long—only an hour or two at best. Who knew what deals bankers traded back and forth, sharing insider information, trading fees, and commissions, especially in "good old" Mississippi. Bankers had no privileges to respect, and money was God. They helped each other when they could from one deal to the next and kept their accounts between themselves. They knew how to keep their mouths shut about their sources better than any newspaper reporters called before Congress. It was a deplorable private pipeline but nothing new.

Two and a half hours later, or slightly longer than he thought it would take, Rosario's banker called his lawyer back. It was a friendly conversation, as well it should be. The lawyer's sister had been married to the banker's first cousin on his mother's side, and the cousin was a well-known Jackson plastic surgeon. The relationship was such, on the female family side, that they were not linked to each other by name. They had a long history of sending each other business well outside the rerouting of others in the bank or the lawyer's firm.

Rosario was right. Helms was the buyer, but he was not the only buyer. Little Miss Trucker was to be a 50 percent owner. They were going to be the new hot couple in town, once Rosario and Julie moved on; because of the noncompete clause, there was little else for them to do businesswise in Jackson.

Miss Trucker was putting up no money. She had more control over her boyfriend than she should have. She was likely shaking him down, at least in a social manner. How long could he expect his marriage to Mrs. Helms to last once Miss Trucker's ownership in the Mansion was out in the open? It meant a $2.5 million gift to her of money that came from Mrs. Helms' family. No married woman would sit still for that, even in Mississippi.

Mrs. Helms was in the Mansion by six-thirty. She passed directly into the Rough Rider Room but did not take her usual reserved table. Instead, she sat at the bar. The theme for the week had already been established several days before. It was military officers, and she had already appeared in a marine corps female major's uniform. Tonight, she was dressed in civilian clothes, albeit a costly five thousand–dollar hand-tailored yellow Chanel suit, which in some social circles, was itself a kind of uniform. Maybe through her own grapevine, she had figured out that it was not to be a regular evening and that she would be invited into Rosario's inner circle, and she did not want to take her place in fantasy clothes.

Rosario was somewhat surprised that Mrs. Helms was not literally in uniform. He greeted her graciously, commenting on how nice she looked. In return, he got her best schoolgirl smile and nothing more. Rosario asked her to join Julie and his friends upstairs for dinner, if she wished, so they could bring her up to date on their last conversation and what they had developed. She smiled again, nodding affirmatively and standing. This smile was no schoolgirl smile but rather a wry, knowing smile. She was indeed joining the inner circle of what she knew to be her husband's enemies. She was coming of age in their conspiracy against him and the others. She was doing so quite willingly. It was time to play her cards, and she was more than ready. She followed Rosario's lead, and up they went in the private rear elevator, saying nothing.

Julie greeted them and showed Mrs. Helms around Rosario's executive suite. Mrs. Helms asked Julie where she stayed; it was obvious to her that none of Julie's items were in the master bedroom or bathroom suite. Julie had not expected her question but was not put off.

"Come on, let me show you."

Julie took her down to the second floor and then to the third floor facilities and gym. Mrs. Helms' face lit up when she saw the training area. Julie was fairly sure Kroper had already signed her up for his private lessons. Mrs. Helms looked happy for the first time, and Julie was not going to disturb the moment. In her own mind, she concluded that Mrs. Helms had not really wanted so much to see her rooms as the gym itself, so she could make her own plans of what to wear, where to change and shower, and what she might need on hand to train.

On the way back up, Julie showed her where the other men stayed on the fourth floor—the spacious kitchen and the one remaining guest room, which was still unoccupied but fully decorated. Mrs. Helms politely paid her compliments for what they had done in the makeover but added still more than compliments. She remarked that, as a child, she had been a church member, so she knew the building as it had been years before. She said the upstairs makeover was more remarkable than the downstairs Mansion itself. Her final remark let it go.

"It's a shame I wouldn't be a half owner."

No one was surprised that she already knew about it on her own. It was clear that Mrs. Helms had her own talkative banker in her pocket, or maybe one of theirs. It didn't matter. She had shown her cards. She was ready, willing, and able to sign up with them, and she was saying so. It was time for dinner.

Dinner was as fine a meal as they could enjoy downstairs. Music filled the room, and the drink was champagne. They had all earned it. The plotting, planning, and hard work had paid off. The games had begun, and it was time for gaiety before closure—whatever that would take or cost. They all spoke freely of times past, the legion, the Mansion, and even the farm, of which Mrs. Helms was yet unaware. Kroper and Louis would take her out the next more morning to show it to her, in case she had to join them or exit by plane if Mr. Helms elected to get ugly with his Klan friends. It was something that was still possible, even highly likely, but not very clever in the face of the proof they had assembled.

Nevertheless, because they knew that closure and likely confrontation were coming, the issue of calling in more men came up again. It was put in terms of meeting a Klan challenge. Better safe than sorry was the order of the day. When it was finally resolved, the decision was no. More men would more likely lead to confrontation and armed violence. They would all be pursued by the law. They had come too far to let it degenerate into a blameworthy killing field. It would be better to take the five million and run to Venezuela (or Cuba) if need be, making the facts public in Judge Barrett's court for a new trial or a discharge of Rosario's conviction. Mrs. Helms thought that, depending on how matters developed, she could defuse the Klansmen with her own disclosures. Words were deemed to be more powerful than weapons and manpower, especially with their exit strategy should all else fail.

CHAPTER THIRTY-SEVEN
The Morning After

Kroper and Louis picked up Mrs. Helms and drove her out to the farm. They took her through all of it, including the security problems, the hidden weapons, the backup cars, and the Cessna. Even as a novice, she seemed to absorb it all.

She talked about how she had known the doctor who had lived there before and had followed his horses. He had been a friend of her parents, and she had known him and his family from the country club set. She had had no idea that he was a weapons collector or that his farm had been so well arranged. She thought the house exquisite, particularly for being so unknown and hidden away while so close to Jackson.

Louis quipped that he would see to it that Rosario gave it to her when they left town, if she didn't go with them. He would throw in the plane too, if she agreed to learn how to fly it. The idea of someone giving her such a lavish present blindsided her. She fell into a laughter and coughing fit, and the two of them joined in.

Back in town, Rosario was signing off, though not with laughter, on the already tightened up contract of sale. He received the nonrefundable earnest money and deposited the million dollars with his bank, leaving instructions with the chief teller's window to have Arnot Sinclair wire it to his Swiss bank in three days. He arranged for a telex to be sent to Hans

Gruber so he would look for it coming in and kindly confirm its receipt. As was his habit, he sent separate instructions to the Swiss bank directing that a ten thousand–dollar check be given to Gruber with a note for him to take a small trip whenever he and his wife wanted. It included a devoted thank-you for Gruber's attention to Rosario's needs. He advised that another four million dollars should follow in a month or less.

That would leave him with about $180,000 in the States to operate with after the closing. Any more funds needed for the staff would be paid directly from Zurich. The remaining banked monies would be drawn down in cash just before the closing. Nothing would be left around for any state court judge to let Mr. Helms tie up, if it came down to disputes with lawyers.

CHAPTER THIRTY-EIGHT

Timing Is Everything

If the planned disclosure were to work, it would happen in only a few days. There was no sense in sorting it out too soon. The title searches and business tax signoffs and a host of other closing documents and affidavits were being finalized well before needed for the Mansion's closing.

No effort was needed to track Vickie Trucker down at her home or the sheriff. Mrs. Helms knew where to find them both. Mr. Helms was around, but not staying much at home much. He, too, was easy to find when his time came. The plan was to start moving forward, only a day or two before the closing. Mr. Helms' tension would be at its highest with so much to do. He was most likely to fumble then if he would at all.

The closing was set for less than two weeks away at the Mansion on a Thursday afternoon. Helms need not be present since he had arranged to presign the sale documents and closing statements, which had been sent a week in advance to Ross Gillmore II for review and final approval, although he had already been through the drafts before and approved them. The finalized originals would be held, pending only the closing.

At the Mansion, it was business as usual, even though the sale put a damper on staff enthusiasm. For the last two weeks, Mr. Helms had sent his own consultants to try to hire staff members, but without success. No one was signing up.

Stephanie was a key to the Mansion's, and she was offered double salary for a year, if she could deliver up to half of the staff at a 10 percent advance of their current salaries. She didn't even try. It wasn't her problem, and she had no intention of working for him. He did not know that there was to be indeterminate ongoing standby pay. The contract did not forbid it, and although it was calculated to undermine any startup by Mr. Helms, it was a topic that he had missed from the outset. The restaurant business had not been his primary goal. Instead, getting rid of Rosario had been the focus, and it was only when Miss Trucker saw her chance to trade up to become Mrs. Helms by slipping into Julie's role that real attention was paid as to how to keep the Mansion going.

Frenchy, Louis, and Kroper were watching the newly arrived wannabe Mrs. Helms in shifts around the clock to make sure they could get to Miss Trucker the moment they wanted to to set the plan in motion. The meeting time had been set for Tuesday afternoon early, even if she didn't know it. The sheriff would be next, once they had her response. Depending on the outcome, they would approach Mr. Helms or let him just dangle instead.

Kroper had trained Mrs. Helms three times in two-hour sessions. For a woman about fifty with a history of no formal exercise program and who was hardly a teetotaler, he found her in remarkably good trim. Obviously, there were some things he didn't know about her past, but upon cooling down at the end of their first session, he found out during their chitchat.

As a child, she had been an avid tennis player and a competing junior. The Helms family compound had a well-maintained gym, a sauna, a whirlpool, and a tennis court. She hit with a pro every day of the week. No one knew.

She sweated the liquor out and was still young enough to overcome the poisonous effects on the body that it deposited in her. Three times a week, she played squash in the afternoons, at various men's clubs, where she was welcome. Mostly, she played with doctors, lawyers, and even judges or her father's friends and their children. The most usual courts she booked were routinely at the Jewish Y, so word of her athletic prowess had not gotten around. She spent an hour each day going through her own exercise routine early in the morning, warming up for the day's sports. She was in a lot better shape than most workout gurus or the one and only Hanoi Jane Fonda. Most real athletes could afford to drink the long night through like Australian marathoners, downing their cases of beer each night before their twenty-six mile runs the next day.

Kroper was impressed and should have been. Here was a woman already hooked on her own endorphin output. There was little he could do for her conditioning-wise. To his own sorrow, he regretted that he had never gone in for party sports, tennis, and squash. Maybe she could give him lessons when it was all over.

This left the topic of divorce. He was supposed to train her, even in a few sessions, to have the strength to file her divorce in timing with the overall disruption of Mr. Helms' life. There was no sense beating around the proverbial bush. It was his topic to develop, and there was no way around it, even if it compromised any ongoing relationship with her. He put the truth to her. Training her was not a ploy, but they were not sure her inner strength was up to a divorce because of her drinking. No one was aware that she was in champion-class condition. How could they have known?

He explained the overall plan of disruption and its intended effects on Helms and her replacement, Miss Trucker. He didn't know if who filed first had anything to do with the trusts, but if it did, she should hold off on starting the divorce. The plan was to bankrupt him and not her to his benefit. He discovered that, without reservation, the funeral homes and properties were held by her, her family, or her family trusts. Mr. Helms would receive no help from them.

If it would help, she was more than ready to file and needed only moral support upon which she could depend—real friendship.

CHAPTER THIRTY-NINE

Getting Down

Tuesday afternoon before the closing came soon enough. It was action time. Mrs. Helms had been at the lawyer's all morning, getting her divorce papers ready for filing and service on her husband later in the day. The filing itself sought an order to immediately end his access to the trust funds, funeral home profits, and casino monies, at least until an audit could be conducted. The terms of the trust were recited, referencing his lack of access to her property once a divorce was at hand. He was shut off with no borrowing power left.

If he was going to close on the Mansion, he would have to use his own money and not hers. It would be close to the skin for him to come up with another four million dollars after the divorce. Worst of all, it would have to come from joint marital assets that they had developed during the marriage. She would get half of a piece of the Mansion in the divorce, even if he could close. She would not stop the closing, because such interference might cost her a denial of her participation in ownership of the Mansion and a claim on their marital assets if the bonding companies had to pay on the letter of credit. What would happen was all up in the air. Nothing was clear, except that their marriage was well over, and she was moving forward.

Kroper and Louis didn't exactly barge in on Miss Trucker at one p.m.

They rang the bell, and she made the mistake of opening the door. At first, she didn't recognize them, but she knew them soon enough after they said they were from the Mansion; they were Rosario's friends. She had seen them there and in the photo array of the staff, since she had been helping Mr. Helms to determine whom to keep. They were certainly not on that list. Oblivious to their purpose but thinking it might advance the cause of keeping some of the staff, she invited them in, offering coffee or tea.

Kroper spoke up, breaking the silence when they were all seated in her living room. There was no sign of her child.

"It's not really a social call, Vickie," Kroper said, calling her by her first name and taking her aback some. It was not very Southern of him.

"Really, why not?" she asked, giving him her best dancer smile.

"It's about our problems—your problems—we came to discuss," spoke up Louis. The good cop/bad cop routine was in play. There was no good cop.

"How can I help you?"

"It's really the other way around, Vickie," Kroper said. He and Louis were playing off each other like a world wrestling championship tag team.

"How so? What could you possibly do for me? I don't even know you."

"It's easy." Louis took the lead while Kroper deferred to him.

"Not to me, it isn't." Her voice was cracking; she no longer sounded so sure of herself.

"Certainly, you remember our good friend, Rosario?"

"Yes."

"He was the one with the bathroom blood when you came forward at the end of his trial. Do you remember how you had seen him the night of the murder?"

"Yes," she said meekly, her voice now in shambles.

"Well, we came to help you about that, Vickie."

"I don't need your help. It's done and over."

"Done, yes. Over, no, I'm afraid, Vickie."

"Please, both of you leave now. We have nothing to discuss," she said, nearly shouting, just short of becoming hysterical.

"Gladly, if you wish, young lady, but then we can't help you. No complaints later on when the chips fall in place, you know."

"I have no chips. What chips?" She no longer seemed to really follow the drift of their conversation; instead she focused only on her head pounding and her adrenalin pumping.

"We have the chips, not you, my dear. Well, you have them too. Now, we all have them."

She began to stand, to protest, to show them out, knowing that it was likely all over for her.

"Why don't you have a look at these papers—the chips—then let us know if you really want us to leave without helping?" While he was speaking, he handed her the documents that Frenchy had pulled off the Internet, knowing it would not take her long to understand them.

She sat and flipped through the pagesthe bank deposits and the charges for the New York shopping trip and the flight. She flipped through them twice more, knowing they were genuine; they were the same as her own. She stayed away from the expected rhetoric about how and where they got them. The point was that they had them; it was a nonissue.

"How can you help me?" She asked, putting it out there.

"Well, first, we have to talk about filling in some details. It helps us answer your question, helps us to know how we can help you best."

"Why should I confess anything to you? What does that get me?"

Not sitting again but turning back to her, Louis started up again.

"You don't get it, young lady, not at all. No applied reasoning. Think about it in overall terms. You set up Rosario. He gets out early and puts a large amount of money into Jackson to get started in business, and he becomes a local hero of sorts. He brings in his friends—yours truly and Kroper. Doesn't that get you going? Who are we? Not who are you, and not even who is Mr. Helms. We've got all of that down. You see the papers. There's no getting around them. A case of perjury—paid perjury, no less—and in a murder case. Very nasty stuff. So where are we? Some Johnnies come lately? No. We are the pipers. Time has come to pay the piper. The price of admission is the topic. Sugar or salt, the hard way or the easier way. The easy way is gone. You used that up when you got involved by doing the bad deed and lying to the judge and jury. Now it's payback time, and the hill of debt will just get steeper and steeper if you want to get uppity, maybe try to treat us like we are stupid, play possum with us, or try to bolt or lie later on down the road."

Kroper gave Louis a "relax" glare and took up the slack himself. He was not friendly to her, but he tightened up on the facts at hand.

"To get to the end of the road, we really don't need your help. We take these documents to Judge Stittin and have Rosario's lawyer ask to open the conviction, vacate it. The judge drags you into it all, and down goes your house of cards. It's time to get someone to raise your child for the next five to ten years, even with good behavior. Judge Stittin will end up sentencing you, and since the crime was about money—your twenty-five thousand dollars down and a $180,000 casino payout—so far, it looks like a long stay to me."

Trucker was silent as a lamb—their lamb ready for slaughter, just to end it all quickly.

"The casino money is gone, and its payback is likely. Even now, no more casino money, but maybe no or little jail with restitution. It's always hard to tell at the start."

"What do you want from me, if you know it all?"

"Cooperation and a more favorable attitude," piped up Louis.

There was little more to say, to sort out. It was all on the table. Time to fish or cut bait. The conversation was done. The ebb and flow of words were becalmed. No one was saying anything. It was her choice, not theirs. They waited her out, and it took a while. She was no longer in a hurry to have them leave. The prolonged silence told them she was thinking it over carefully, and for that, she needed time.

Kroper clocked her silence in at about four and a half minutes. At five, he would have stood to leave. It never got to that point. She was done a half minute early.

She kept it simple; her sole reply was, "Okay." More than that would have been redundant and likely untrustworthy, if she blabbered along. "Okay" was just answer enough, and the right answer. Future trickery aside, she had agreed.

"Now what?"

"We get it all down in black and white on paper with a lawyer. It avoids problems later and you can't change your mind, claiming you were coerced or threatened by us or Rosario. It would be hard to do, especially with the documents you have seen. Still, it's the best way. End it and take yourself out of the loop as best as possible."

Kroper followed up carefully, wanting her to understand it all so she knew that she was caught.

"Let me help you along, save you some time. If you are thinking, say yes now and have Mr. Helms get you out later and ride into the sunset with him and his money, forget about it. Mrs. Helms is on our team already. As we speak, she is filing for a divorce from Mr. Wonderful. The trusts and casino shares and funeral home properties are hers. It all goes back to her. He is out, and pretty much on his own. He still has to come up with four million dollars on a secured pledge to buy the Mansion, and he has no workers. He has no rich wife anymore and no money except perhaps yours and your credit. If the course of true love is going to run strong, now is the time. You support him, you bankrupt yourself and go to jail standing next to him. How does that sound?"

"Where do I get a lawyer? Who is going to help dig me out of this?

"It's time for you to find one and have him contact Rosario's lawyer. We can't do that for you. It's better just to hire one and let our lawyer fill him in. If he says he will get you out of all of it, then you need to improve your lawyer selection skills and get a new legal eagle. It's not going away."

They said their goodbyes, promising to call her early the next afternoon either to end it or move on without her. It was very clear. As the door shut, they could hear her mewing turn to sobbing of despair. The tears of the woman didn't move them. She had made her bed. Now she could sleep in it.

As far as Kroper was concerned, she was way ahead of the curve. He had wanted to take the three of them—her, Mr. Helms, and the sheriff—up in the Cessna and have her confess and throw them all out at three thousand feet over the ocean. The problem was that it was no solution. They would be missed. Otherwise, he still thought it was a pretty good idea. It hadn't left his mind yet.

CHAPTER FORTY

Eight Ball in the Corner Pocket

The game was winding down. The rack of balls was gone, and it was time to call the final eight ball shot. All of the earlier balls had fallen into place. It was time to end it.

The sheriff was easy to find. How much he knew or didn't fess up to no longer mattered. They had the goods. They could prove the twenty-five thousand–dollar first payment and his profit checks from the casino that he needed to pay back and have ended. His winning hand was folded.

In a way, his harm was greatest. He had violated the public trust solely for gain. He had ignored his vow of office to honor justice and the code of law. Rosario could not have been convicted if the sheriff had come forward with the truth. He had done it for greed, not passion or the protection of family. He was the greatest offender. His debt of repayment was the largest due.

Within an hour of leaving Miss Trucker's house, Kroper and Louis caught up with him at home. It took them less than fifteen minutes to lay it all out to him. They thought he was relieved in a way. It seemed almost as though he had been waiting for this day of exposure while he plied himself with the benefits of his crime, the money already spent and gone.

He got the same package that Vickie had, including proof of his initial twenty-five thousand–dollar check and of his casino distributions.

They told him outright that there would be no deal. He could disclose it all himself, or they would. He had a few days to resolve it on his own. No other multiple choice solutions existed. He looked sickened. It was as though he had known the day of reckoning would come but had never focused on when it would be.

When their conversation was done, Kroper and Louis left. There was nothing to say, nothing to debate. For him, it was over. He would lose his office, pension, and freedom—he would almost certainly receive a long prison term for violating the public's trust. He would spend his term in jail fearful of being killed as a police official. Even if there was a large chance that he would be killed in jail, that alone would not stop his stiff sentence from being imposed.

It was late afternoon, and Kroper and Louis returned to the Mansion to report and to participate in the nightly affairs. The early-bird regulars were beginning to filter in, and they went to the Rough Rider Room to join in and relax. The mood was the usual nightly festive spirit. Because the night was still very early and not in full swing, because it was before opening time, the one overhead bar television was still on the news channel the staff watched as they set up. It was no more than an hour or so since they had left the sheriff's home.

The television showed an age old crime scene with the coroner's van and yellow-taped home. They didn't even recognize it at once, but it was unnecessary. The coroner was plainly reporting that the sheriff had been found dead by his wife. It was an apparent suicide. He had swallowed the gun. They made no mention of a suicide note. There never would be one.

The death would be ruled a suicide. He would get a police officer's funeral, keep his pension for his family, and avoid public scrutiny and embarrassment, and there would be no payback of ill-gotten monies. The sheriff's exit strategy card had been played. It was a done deal.

Kroper and Louis had two drinks instead of only the one they had planned on. It was a good day's work.

CHAPTER FORTY-ONE

Last Man Standing

A scant two days after the sheriff's death, Mr. Helms' personal empire collapsed. His police influence was gone. His marriage was over publically. His benefits from Mrs. Helms' trusts and casino interests were finished. His girlfriend was gone and posed a likely jail threat to him should she make disclosures. He no longer had any access to the sums of money she liked and that kept her friendly. Worst of all, he had defaulted on his purchase of the Mansion and lost the million-dollar deposit. The letter of credit for four million would be called, and he would lose the security that he had put up for it. There would be no purchase funding. He had been had. Everything had all been turned around on him overnight. He was now not only morally bankrupt but financially too.

Somehow the word that he was up against it had been revealed to the Klan. He didn't know how and never would. It could not have been Rosario, because he did not travel in those circles. It could have been his wife, but she had no use for the Klan. He thought it was one of the bankers or lawyers, but it didn't matter. He would never prove it and to whom would he anyway? He was surrounded by alpha males who were looking to take over as grand wizard now that he was labeled a risk and no longer trustworthy of leadership because of his own problems. He would not even be a contender. He could muster no armies against Rosario. There were no legions to follow him. His reign was over.

At best, it was back to the funeral home to sell his caskets, dress the dead, and drive the burial car to pick up the bodies at the hospital back door. He wasn't even sure he could keep his clientele or maintain his professional reputation with all of his influence and money gone. He was already a broken man and, predictably, would become more and more reclusive, overwhelmed, and alcohol addicted, like so many others in the burial game. It wasn't death overnight but a long, gradual, daily decline into despair, ill health, and mental disorder. It was, however, quite predictable and due him. The punishment fit the crime: a slow and horrible self-imposed death.

Vickie Tucker was faring somewhat better. She had her freedom and her child. She had youth and good looks still on her side. She had had a taste of the good life, even if she was back to living on one thousand dollars per week. In a way, it was redeeming and refreshing for her. She no longer had to smile and cozy up to Helms, being his whore in public to get her big piece of the pie that would never come. In a way, she had been able to buy herself back cheaply. She had escaped the far worse fates of the sheriff and Mr. Helms. She had gotten off cheaply.

She kept her part of the bargain. She gave her lawyer a full statement of her participation in the cover-up details and anonymously assigned any casino interest she had to the parents of the dead children. Due to the attorney-client privilege, he was barred from disclosing her confession unless certain events occurred. If she died, he could do so, or if the statute on perjury of five years had run out and Rosario made a specific request in order to clear his name. In that event, the documents would be submitted, sealed, to Judge Stittin for his determination.

Less than a month later, she was back up on her own two feet, feeling self-cleansed, reconstituted, and good about herself, knowing she had reached out for the gold ring and dropped it. The truth be told, she was glad she had taken the chance. So what if it had failed? It had not turned out sour; it was just another lost opportunity. Most girls with gumption and of questionable background would have tried, like so many other

Vegas-type showgirls or Hollywood actresses before her. Her final thoughts were that it had not changed her or made her a bad person. She was still hale, healthy, and a good mother. She could also still stop a man at twenty feet and have him stare at her like a deer blinded by car lights at night. She had not weathered in her appearance. She was still really charming and pretty. The whole journey had been vacation enough. Now, it was time for her to get back on the eligibility shelf.

She went back to dancing and even became somewhat of a headliner, especially in the redneck bars of Mississippi, where she danced under the name of Miss Klan Klox Kotie. The boys knew who she was and who she had been. They lined up to stuff their fives, tens, and twenties while she tried to separate the wheat from the chaff, still looking for another gold ring.

CHAPTER FORTY-TWO
Aftermath

It had all happened and ended so suddenly. The balls of life had all fallen into place. What had been only a plan had borne fruit. The game had been well played by Rosario and his friends. They had prepared for war and sued for and won their peace of mind. They had sought revenge and gotten it. They had risked getting dirty themselves (with murder, if need be) and stayed clean. They had sought just rewards and found them. They had worked hard and won the game, sweating along the way but not becoming overwhelmed. Most of all, they had become a family, deeply bonded like blood kin to each other. It was the best reward.

Time had told their outcome, which had far outweighed the effort. They had delivered justice where it was due and been paid back handsomely themselves. Rosario could have stuck to the medium of democracy and taken their votes on how to wind down. He didn't do so, rather following only his own plan. He had started it and would end it. He didn't want any arguments about who got what, because they thought he was being too generous.

He had sent the million dollar deposit back to Switzerland to repay his investment funds. He had tipped his banker ten thousand dollars for his own frolic and family fun.

Kroper and Mrs. Helms had gone from personal trainer and friend to being an item. Kroper was still bloodthirsty, but even in a few brief months, she mellowed his soul. He was more elastic in his thoughts and personality. Obviously, he could not compete with Mrs. Helms' fortune, but at his age, Kroper had no need to prove himself or his strengths.

Rosario gave Kroper the right to use the farm as his own for the rest of his life. If he married Mrs. Helms, they were to get the ownership. Mrs. Helms would not be motivated to marry for just another piece of property, but in the end, Rosario did not want to take away the memories in the house that she and Kroper would share if married. Kroper was a tough legionnaire, and many of them were healthy well into their nineties. He still had several decades to go, and by then, Mrs. Helms would be nearly eighty. Rosario wished them a long life together and wanted to facilitate it if he could.

Frenchy and Louis were another matter. He doubted that they would stay long in Jackson. It would be back to their hideouts at home for them to ruminate over good memories and camaraderie, waiting until the next life event mustered them up. Other than friendship, there was little else they needed. To Rosario, that was of no moment. The Mansion was a gold mine of its own. It took in tens of thousands of dollars weekly. He fixed a rent of two hundred thousand dollars for the property, to be paid in equal halves to each of them for life.

Stephanie received 10 percent of the profit, Rosario's apartment to reside in, and general management of the Mansion. Julie received a 20 percent ownership and the rental income if anything happened to Frenchy or Louis. The remaining 70 percent in profit was to be paid out as an operating bonus to the employees who had served with him for the first few years and then to the workers still on staff thereafter in addition to their salaries.

He took nothing for himself but the pride in his own deals. He did keep the four million–dollar letter of credit but did not transfer ownership to Mr. Helms. It was a Mexican stand-off. Helms could sue for it, but Rosario would bring out his crimes; their positions were solid and not moving. So in the end, Rosario still owned the business and the real estate, but he was far too young and far too wealthy—at more than thirty million dollars—to be concerned about any details for making money for himself from the overall operation.

Rosario remained unsettled in one area. It was not something he could direct, even if it was his own future. He sure wasn't staying in Jackson any longer. He had no reason to push Vickie Trucker into premature disclosure at her own risk just to clear his name. He didn't need to, especially if he was going back into the legion.

Rosario just wasn't certain. He loved the legion. It had helped him a great deal. No one loved the battlefield, but he didn't fear it. The camaraderie was a large boost to him, and he enjoyed practicing rough-and-ready surgery. He would not take up a regular commercial hospital routine just to become a family man. He was not going to sell out his life for more big bucks he didn't need.

The biggest problem was Julie. He didn't want her to leave him. But he couldn't control her decision. Her 20 percent, without being committed to work, would likely bring her about a million in income a year, so she didn't need to roost with him. Moreover, if she tried and it didn't work, she could leave at any time. The best he could do was ask her to leave with him when he went back to Zurich to sort it all out in the short or long run. At least one solution to it was clear. Only time would tell.